Praise for *Ask Y*

"When Kitty Stryker tugs on the thread (sive power structures start to unravel. This workbook gets down to the fundamental principles of how humans need to treat one another. Taking its own methology to heart, it offers no authoritative answers, just smart, emotionally astute questions that could upend how you think about the problem of other people."

—Alison Bechdel, author of *Dykes to Watch Out For* and *Fun Home*

"These conversations on consent are essential for building healthy dynamics in all of our relationships, not just sexual ones. *Ask Yourself* offers us a tool towards understanding our ongoing relationship with consent beyond just 'yes' and 'no.'"

—Andy Duran, education director, Good Vibrations and Babeland

"This workbook is an essential resource for building a culture that is based on mutual respect, dignity, safety, and pleasure. It is, ultimately, about how we care for each other. It's an invaluable resource for making sure we build identities, communities, and a society that is committed to making sure we do."

—Soraya Chemaly, author of *Rage Becomes Her: The Power of Women's Anger*

"I'm very grateful for the work of serious activist-educators like Stryker, and her new book is exactly what's needed in this moment. It's a practical workbook that takes the reader, step by step, from the inside out, into a thorough awareness of their own personal definition, need and application of consent. If that sounds heavy, it is—as it should be. It's also profound, lovely, timely, universal, and highly actionable. One comes away from this book with a much deeper understanding of the nuanced and evolving idea of consent, a clearer understanding of one's own place within this landscape and, perhaps most importantly, the tools to be of service to others. This is a vital text."

—Alex Winter, actor, *Bill & Ted's Excellent Adventure*

"Whether you're looking for help setting and hearing interpersonal boundaries, exploring and communicating your sexual desires, or understanding the nuance of consent, *Ask Yourself* provides honest, trauma-informed information and practices to build up our toolboxes as safer, happier, more authentic sexual beings."

—Dr. Melissa A. Fabello, author of *Appetite: Sex, Touch, and Desire in Women with Anorexia*

"*Ask Yourself* combines candid commentary from experts in the field with journal prompts designed to make the learning and unlearning process feel contained and supported. I would recommend this workbook to anyone who's ready to dive deeper and build a stronger understanding of what it takes to build and maintain a true culture of consent."

—Anne Hodder-Shipp, sex and relationships educator and author of *Speaking From the Heart: 18 Languages for Modern Love*

"This is a f*cking good book!"
—Nicole Byer, actor, comedian, and host of Netflix's *Nailed It*

"*Ask Yourself* is a much-needed resource for individuals and groups to collectively think through the complex dynamics that shape how we conduct ourselves in all aspects of life. Stryker has no illusions about how difficult that work is, nor any doubt about its urgency if we are to make safer communities today and build a new world tomorrow."

—Mark Bray, history professor and author of *Antifa: The Anti-Fascist Handbook*

"Whether you're already an advocate looking to further your understanding or new to the concept of consent culture and bettering the power dynamics in your everyday life, the perspectives and tools discussed within are not just worth reading, but worth returning to many times thereafter."

—Matthew Mercer, voice actor and Game Master for *Dungeons & Dragons* web series *Critical Role*

ASK
YOURSELF

ALSO BY KITTY STRYKER

Ask: Building Consent Culture

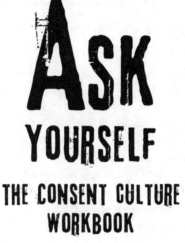

Ask
YOURSELF
THE CONSENT CULTURE WORKBOOK

Kitty Stryker

THORNAPPLE PRESS

Thornapple Press
300 – 722 Cormorant Street
Victoria, BC V8W 1P8 Canada
press@thornapplepress.ca

Thornapple Press is a brand of Talk Science to Me Communications Inc. and the successor to Thorntree Press. Thornapple Press's business offices are located in the traditional, ancestral and unceded territories of the ləkʷəŋən and W̱SÁNEĆ peoples.

Cover design by Jeff Werner and HardestWalk
Interior design by Jeff Werner
Author photo by L. M. deLeon
Substantive editing by Andrea Zanin
Copy-editing by Hazel Boydell
Proofreading by Heather van der Hoop

Library and Archives Canada Cataloguing in Publication
Title: Ask yourself : the consent culture workbook / Kitty Stryker.
Names: Stryker, Kitty, 1984- author.
Identifiers:
    Canadiana (print) 20220424446 | Canadiana (ebook) 20220424497 |
    ISBN 9781778242007 (softcover) | ISBN 9781778242014 (EPUB)
Subjects: LCSH: Interpersonal relations. | LCSH: Autonomy (Psychology)
    | LCSH: Sexual consent. | LCSH: Power (Social sciences)
Classification: LCC HM1111 .S77 2023 | DDC 302/.1—dc23

10 9 8 7 6 5 4 3 2 1

Printed in Canada.

This work is dedicated to Tobias Slater, who strived toward creating consent culture and its accompanying accountability, even when it was messy and hard. Perhaps especially then.

He taught me to be vulnerable and how to have fun again—he believed in me when I didn't believe in anything. He encouraged me to pitch this workbook. I wish he were here to see it published.

GNU, Tobias.

The past can hurt. But the way I see it, you can either run from it, or learn from it.
—Rafiki, *The Lion King*

Contents

Acknowledgments

Everyone I've ever met, whether our interactions were positive or negative, has influenced the content of this workbook and how I think about consent culture more widely. But there are a few people I especially wanted to thank:

To my publisher and friend, Eve Rickert, for believing in me and trusting in my passion and skill. Her faith gave me the courage to keep doing this work, and to be raw and open and honest as I do it.

To the people who contributed their personal stories to this book in order to give readers a diversity of opinions and perspectives to help them inform their own choices.

To Wagatwe Wanjuki, who said yes to writing a foreword for this workbook, and who has been doing instrumental, tireless work in the world of anti-rape activism. She is an inspiration and working alongside her remains an honor and a privilege.

To my mum and dad, who raised me as a feminist, as an anarchist, and as someone who believes fiercely in mutual aid. They taught me to care, to respect my heart, and to fight back against injustice.

To my sister Avens for reminding me of my bias and encouraging me to think critically about these issues, gently nudging me to communicate them to a wider audience.

To my friends Kat and Edie "Keepsfire," who sat patiently with me through multiple phone calls of panic and uncertainty as I hammered out the questions and format of this workbook.

To my platonic life partner, Quin, and my sponsor, Nazelah, for helping me stay grounded throughout this process. Also to my D&D groups, who gave me a sober community.

To the many people who shared the drafts with their friends, students, and communities, and helped me fine-tune this workbook into the best thing it could be. I appreciate you taking this for a test run and giving me strong feedback.

To people doing consent work, such as Sarah Casper (Comprehensive Consent), A.V. Flox (*Disrupting the Bystander*), Nadine Thornhill (Make It About Race), Betty Martin (*The Art of Receiving and Giving*), Sar Surmick (The Consent Academy), Jenny Wilson (Consent Culture UK), Indigo Dawn (The Connection Institute). They all do incredible, inspiring work I learn a lot from. This book is better in part thanks to them, and I appreciate it!

And, most especially, to the sex educators who came before me, who welcomed me into the fold and gave me the strength to turn a blog entry into a movement. Carol Queen, Robert Lawrence, Jay Wiseman, Patrick Califia—you were there at the very beginning, reassuring me that what I was doing was needed and important. You are the foundation on which I stand. I am so grateful to have you in my life.

Foreword

WAGATWE WANJUKI

*A writer, educator, and digital strategist who is empowering
survivors and helping communities improve how they
prevent and respond to gender-based violence.*

As an anti-rape educator and survivor, I've always had a
complicated relationship with the mainstream narratives
around consent.

When I first learned about consent as a young adult, it was
helpful in my healing journey. Coming of age amidst evangel-
ical purity culture had distorted my sense of autonomy and
boundary violation. Consent education was the springboard
for coming to terms with my own survivorhood and starting
to do the work to recover.

My discomfort comes from the ways consent education
has been treated as a silver bullet in rape prevention—especially on college campuses. Despite being a peer consent
educator in the early 2000s, I found common phrases like
"consent is sexy" earnest and well-intentioned, but insuffi-
cient in adequately addressing campus rape culture.

My discomfort initially lay in the hidden message of this
approach: *Rape is merely caused by ignorance of consent, so
we just have to educate the poor, confused (potential) rapists
to solve rape culture!* I wish creating a rape-free society was
that easy, but a quick look at the history of rape in the United

States shows otherwise. While popular consent education treats rape as an individual problem, it hides how sexual assault is a societal problem sustained by inequality and toxic cultural norms.

This individualistic lens reinforces the myth of the bumbling college rapist who is somehow simultaneously brilliant enough to attend a top university but must be coddled and treated as a blank slate when we're discussing something as serious as rape. Approaching rape with this mindset is a gift to rape culture; treating major consent violations as mistakes of ignorance prevents getting to the root of the problem.

It honestly felt like an excuse to limit our conception of prevention of campus sexual assault to *awareness*. It's a lot more comfortable for both administrators and fellow students to believe they have a few ignorant people making mistakes instead of violent rapists in their community.

Years later, I found more information that validated my discomfort. I discovered research citing the lack of empirical evidence of consent education's effectiveness as rape prevention* despite colleges and organizations spending thousands on materials disseminating these messages, especially during sexual assault awareness month. I read about the history of rape in the United States and how the legal system, which guides our concept of consent, used to deem Black women like me unrapable. Inequity is written into the foundation of how we're first taught about consent. Its limited legal meaning has *always* been used to justify oppression.

---

* Melanie Ann Beres. "Rethinking the Concept of Consent for Anti-Sexual Violence Activism and Education." *Feminism & Psychology* 24, no. 3 (2014): 373–389.

Despite my ambivalence, consent education helped me feel confident claiming victimhood despite my rape not fitting the archetype of a stranger attacking me in a dark alley. With the right framing, consent can be a very helpful tool for people like me: trauma survivors who had to *really* learn about our right to our own bodies and garner that knowledge and strength from scratch. That's why I love that this workbook was created. I wish I knew about the concept of consent culture in my early college days as an anti-rape activist fighting for better sexual assault policies. The problem isn't consent—it's our limited cultural understanding and subsequent devaluing of consent in everyday life.

I love that survivors creating meaning out of injustice and rage is written into consent culture's creation story. While *legal* sexual consent was not designed to protect me as a Black woman, I can still find meaning in its principles and build on it—which is exactly what this workbook enables readers to do.

As a Black feminist who always uses an intersectional lens, I emphasize how a power-conscious analysis is *crucial* to discussing consent productively. Consent culture encourages that by offering a new way to understand our relationships to individuals, society, and ourselves.

Ask Yourself provides a much-needed reset in popular conversations about consent. It shows how the "personal is political"—whether we acknowledge it or not. Our personal experiences are shaped by systems of oppression designed to hoard power among a privileged few. Heteropatriarchy, white supremacy, and capitalism all work to normalize coercion so we don't see how unjust the status quo is. If oppressed classes discovered how important consent is *beyond* sex, they'd clearly see how much it's denied to us because it's profitable for inequality's biggest beneficiaries. A consent culture is a direct threat to the oppressive status quo—and it starts with us.

While social media has brought unprecedented popularity of feminism, I often worry the term has been watered down through a game of telephone involving billions. After the explosion of #MeToo, I've made a point to remind people following my content that feminism shouldn't just be about pointing fingers at other people to condemn them. It should also be a guide for ourselves by setting values and goals around how we want to move in everyday life. This workbook helps make that possible by providing a nonjudgmental, structured space for self-reflection and learning.

I'm honored to introduce this fantastic resource and hope it inspires you to consider consent in ways that bring us together while recognizing our different experiences. Oppression thrives on our disconnection to ourselves and to each other, but these pages are an insightful guide into *how* we can fight that disconnection, making us better prepared to build safer communities and a better world.

— Long Beach, California

May 15, 2022

Glossary

There are many ways to define the following concepts, but here is a brief summary of each in my own words, from my perspective.

Accountability: Taking ownership of your choices and actions without defensiveness. Often accountability is a combination of acknowledgment in words, changing behaviors, and making amends in clearly defined ways when appropriate.

Boundaries: A clear space or limit between you and another person, where you begin and others end. Boundaries can be physical, emotional, sexual, temporal, or material. They can be how close you're willing to get to someone else, and also where you draw the line. A "soft" boundary is one that's a little flexible or fuzzy, while a "hard" boundary is clear-cut.

Calling in: Telling someone in private that something they said or did was harmful. Calling in can be effective when there is trust that your individual disapproval is enough to encourage change, as it feels a little more gentle than calling out. However, it does require more of your time and labor as you are on your own. Power dynamics can make this uncomfortable if the person doing the calling in has less clout than the person they're addressing.

Calling out: Telling someone in public that something they said or did was harmful. Calling out can be effective when calling in hasn't worked, when you feel you need witnesses to your call for accountability, or to demonstrate the community's disapproval. Calling out can lead to defensiveness and aggression on the part of the person being called out, and it can lead to uneven consequences that end up impacting marginalized people more.

Consent culture: A social structure focusing on increasing the opportunities for people to opt in (or opt out) of situations. Consent culture is about moving toward centering consent in interactions, rather than avoiding violation. It's about treating autonomy as sacrosanct and boundaries as valuable information to be respected.

Entitlement culture: A social structure in which we arrogantly operate under the impression that other people owe us unreasonable privileges. I prefer to use this term instead of "rape culture" because I feel it more accurately gets to the root of the problem—people with social advantages feeling they deserve something from others because of that power.

FRIES: Shorthand coined by Planned Parenthood when assessing consent. The FRIES model asks if the consent is:
- Freely given
- Reversible
- Informed
- Enthusiastic
- Specific

Marginalization: When certain groups of people are denied access to basic services or opportunities because they are deemed powerless or unimportant. This often goes hand in hand with discrimination, particularly for minorities, and can be related to ethnicity, economic circumstance, gender, sexual orientation, immigration status, physical or mental ability, weight, age, and many other factors. People who are marginalized often experience multiple points of marginalization.

Rape culture: A social structure in which sexual violence (particularly against people who experience misogyny) is normalized, excused away, and dismissed in the media, in the legal system, and/or in the culture at large. Often in a rape culture, victims are blamed for their assaults, and the onus is on avoiding rape instead of on potential rapists not abusing people.

Red flag: A warning sign that something needs to be dealt with or that a problem needs to be addressed. While this term is often used for assessing others (especially in relationships), in this workbook I use it to encourage recognizing your own, internal red flags that tell you that something isn't right, such as feeling queasy or avoiding an interaction. It isn't necessarily a dealbreaker in this context, but rather a sign to stop and reflect on how you feel, what's going on, and what you need.

Restorative justice: An ideal about justice that offers the possibility that someone who does harm can learn, feel empathy, and seek to be accountable for that harm. It seeks to center the victim and give them an active role in the process, rather than relying on an outside corrupt criminal justice system that prefers punishment, retribution, and stigma. Restorative justice is an ideal to work toward, in my opinion, rather than a concrete formula.

Social advantages: Special, unasked for, and unearned positive treatment or value offered only to specific groups by nature of their identity (or perceived identity). It is the counterpart to marginalization. Also called "privilege."

Trigger: A reminder of past trauma, often leading to re-experiencing that trauma in some capacity. Triggers vary wildly, and reactions to them can be internally or externally expressed through dissociation, flashbacks, and distress. Triggers are often referred to in relation to substance abuse or PTSD, but they can also be related to other mental health issues.

Introduction

*Content warning: this book contains discussion of
sexuality, boundary violations, substance use, sexual
assault, abuse, trauma, and other complicated topics*

I can't fully remember when I started to rant to my London
friends about the need for some sort of opposite to the
phrase "rape culture." This is in part because it was over ten
years ago, in part because the beginning discussions were
offline (back when we talked to each other face to face),
and, frankly, in part because my rants were usually fueled
by wine. I do remember, though, that I felt in my gut that
the way in which we were discussing consent prioritized
violations of it—behaviors and situations we wanted to
move *away from*. There wasn't really a pithy way to discuss
what we wanted to move *toward*, what we wanted to center.
As a second-generation anarchist (thanks, mum and dad), I
was accustomed to having big ideals that were hard to mate-
rialize, but I felt like when it came to this issue, a framework
was possible and necessary.

I never could have guessed how far we would come, and
yet how far we have left to go.

The History

As far as I can tell, very few people who write about "consent culture" as an ideal now know that it came from the BDSM community. I'm rarely mentioned, and Cliff Pervocracy, another early adopter, isn't mentioned at all despite writing one of the first online explanations of what a consent culture could look like on his blog, *The Pervocracy,* in a post aptly titled "Consent Culture."

That I am rarely mentioned isn't terribly surprising given that much of my writing on the topic was devastated by online censorship pushes—Blogspot and Tumblr both ended up nuking a lot of my work in their widespread "anti-obscenity" cleanups. One of the first mentions I can find is in a 2012 Salon article, "When Safewords Are Ignored," which covers a consent culture fundraiser that M.M. (who no longer wishes to be connected with the project) and I threw to fund an educational tour for our Safe/Ward workshop. With some hardcore digging, I found an interview with the *San Francisco Bay Guardian* titled "The bad kind of pain: Kitty Stryker talks sexual abuse in the BDSM community" that mentions our first workshop in August 2011. Thomas Macauley Miller credits me and M.M. with really pushing the conversation forward in the post "There's A War On Part 1: Trouble's Been Brewing" on his blog *Yes Means Yes.* Today, the Google alerts I get that mention the phrase "consent culture" are often schools or workplaces who would likely be horrified to know the origin story.

Well, here's the real history, as best I can piece it together.

I was eighteen when I went to my very first kink event. I had read several books about BDSM (an acronym for bondage, dominance, submission, and sadomasochism) and felt excited, inspired, and secure in how often they discussed consent as a cornerstone of the lifestyle. "Safe, sane, and consensual" was the phrase used in the workshops and on the websites.

I was nineteen when I moved to the San Francisco Bay Area, one of the epicenters of leather culture. I volunteered for events and was soon running my own. I became a professional dominatrix and full-service sex worker in my early twenties and a sex educator by my mid-twenties, throwing events in San Francisco and London, touring and teaching.

Bored by the kinky parties I saw available in London, I started Kinky Salon London under the tutelage of Polly Superstar, founder of Kinky Salon San Francisco. A "sexy arty party" that had a cabaret, a video booth, silly costumes, and cozy play spaces, Kinky Salon London became a space for me to try new ways of running a kink event. I tried out techniques that could weave accountability for each other into the fabric of the event itself. It was challenging and exciting, and I created lifelong bonds with the people who took the journey with me.

And yet I was holding a terrible secret. My years in the leather scene were tainted by men—pillars of the community—who had sexually assaulted me. I kept quiet about it because we were in a community focused on consent, right? The fault therefore must be mine, for not safewording (using an agreed-upon stop word), or for not saying no correctly, whatever that meant. I had seen other women get pushed out of the scene for speaking up against their abusers, and so, scared I would lose my friends and my livelihood, I kept silent.

It was when that silence broke that consent culture as a movement was born.

I was living in the Bay Area for the summer. One warm night, I got to talking to one of my friends, M.M. about how often our boundaries had been violated within a BDSM context, and how we were told it was "just part of the process." We knew that no community should normalize violating consent as an education tool—especially a community that outwardly projected consent being the line between "what it is that we do" and abuse. As kinksters ourselves, we had experienced the stigma that we couldn't possibly consent to kinky power play, even something as benign as erotic spanking. As sex workers, we had experienced the stigma that our work was inherently objectifying and that we couldn't consent to that either. While we pushed back against that second-wave feminist mindset, arguing that we were the experts on what we did and did not consent to, we privately discussed how the truth was much more complicated.

M.M. and I realized that we wanted to offer a critique of the idea that the BDSM community actually practiced what it preached, while also critiquing the idea that kink was somehow inherently misogynist. As we talked about it with other friends, we began to realize our experiences were sadly not unique. I was living half of my life in San Francisco, and half in London. Both of the kinky communities I was active in seemed to be experiencing this problem. Once the dam had burst, the stories were overwhelming.

I knew I wanted to make this less of a one-time workshop and more of a movement. I was a social media marketer by trade, so I knew I needed a catchy yet descriptive name, a logo that would look good on stickers and shirts, and a website of content. I knew I didn't want to focus on the negative—I felt that the Kink Anti-Rape Campaign put too much emphasis on what we wanted to move away from, and not what we wanted to move toward. I heard BDSM communities talk about consent a lot—we had phrases like "safe, sane, and consensual" and "risk-aware consensual kink"—but it very quickly became clear that there were a lot of forms of abuse happening, from domestic abuse to microaggressions, and I wanted to embrace discussion of those topics as well as sexual abuse. I wanted to cultivate something about the culture itself.

After trying a few phrases on for size, and many bottles of wine later, in July 2011 the first logo for the Consent Culture Project came into existence. It was two Cs, one on top of the other, with a hole-filled paddle filling the empty space on the right of the letters. Designed by one of my London friends, Tallulah Ker-Oldfield, it was meant to symbolize the first frontier of the "consent culture movement"—the kink communities I spent much of my time in. That project encapsulated several workshops and a bunch of posts online, where I began to ask questions about how liberated we truly were in the BDSM scene. And, as I hoped, the Consent Culture Project fanned the flames of a movement.

I've done a fair amount of research, curious if that project was the first use of the term "consent culture." I think I coined the term, but since these conversations happen both online and in person, it's hard to be certain. Still, I can share the reason why I started using the phrase. I was raised in a world that talked a lot about rape culture, how awful it was, and how we needed to avoid it. But I wanted to focus people's attention on what they *could do* instead. What was the counterpart to rape culture? What was the opposite? Consent culture.

A recent book discusses how consent culture is dangerously limiting, arguing that feminism's use of consent as a buzzword fails to acknowledge the ways in which our consent is complicated by the society in which we live, both in and out of the bedroom. Amusingly, I completely agree, and many of my and Cliff's early writing on the topic delved deeply into what consent really means under a white supremacist capitalist patriarchy. I refused to accept simplifications like "safe, sane, and consensual" or "yes means yes," and that eventually got me ostracized from the kink community.

As a queer, fat, disabled survival-sex worker, I knew how dangerous—and dismissive—such brevity could be, and I didn't want to be quiet about it. I had seen how much bad behavior hid behind "safe, sane, and consensual" without any real definition of what we meant when we said those words. Whose safety? What are the limitations of that safety? Who gets to decide what is and isn't sane? What is the line for someone being coerced versus willing versus eager? "Safe, sane, and consensual" is all well and good, but a lot of the kink behaviors I witnessed would not have passed that test if shown to the average person. Agency and autonomy were a big part of the puzzle.

The concept of consent culture was born from protective and reactive anger at our experiences as people who experience misogyny, especially as people who experience misogyny with multiple marginalizations. And we knew, even then, that it wasn't just for us, or even just referring to sex. As activists who were also deeply entrenched in anti-racist work, fighting cissexist feminism, advocating for sex workers' rights, and engaging in many other battles, we were incredibly aware of the ways in which power dynamics, coercion, and informed consent related to discussions outside of the erotic context to which we originally applied the term "consent culture."

What happened next is something marginalized activists see a lot—the work you do hits the mainstream and you end up being deemed too queer, too weird, too sexual, too unmarketable to be connected to it. Soon enough, you're written out of your own activism. This is, I suppose, the inherent danger when certain causes become popular. We've seen this with callout culture, which has a very specific history within Black communities of restorative and transformative justice but which has been reduced to online complaints. We see it in pole-dancing classes being given in the suburbs while sex workers continue to lose bank accounts and social media platforms. When a concept becomes popular and turns into a buzzword, it comes at a cost—the cost of losing the context.

Ask: Building Consent Culture

In 2017, I edited *Ask: Building Consent Culture*, an anthology that tried to pull the original context of consent culture back to the forefront by centering marginalized voices, particularly the Black, Indigenous, transgender, and disabled people who often found themselves tokenized in feminist conversations. I wanted to fill the book with their thoughts and experiences, but also wanted to be sure that I didn't push anyone to focus their writing on their marginalizations unless *they* wanted to.

Making the process of contributing to the book opt-in and flexible was incredibly important to me. I wanted to model the consent culture I believed was possible, and what better way than by doing it with my own book? I wanted to model what I wanted to see in the world: a white woman using her platform to step back and let others step forward.

While I was editing *Ask*, the United States had just elected Donald Trump—a serial and vocally unrepentant sexual assaulter—as President. Being an anarchist who feels somewhat repulsed by nationalism, I didn't feel betrayed by my country, but rather disappointed in being proved right about my distaste. It was disheartening to see someone who proudly displayed violent misogyny, racism, ableism, and other bigotries be raised to a position of power and privilege and to see how much support he got. Trump's election and the rise of blatant white supremacy fired me up to ensure that *Ask* offered up a diversity of voices and perspectives often shunned in other outlets.

It also made me realize how important it was to talk about consent culture outside of the realm of sexuality. While #MeToo was an ongoing push started in 2006 by longtime Black activist Tarana Burke to raise awareness of women being abused, it only found viral recognition and support in 2017 thanks to a white actress, Alyssa Milano. Burke was often merely called a founder of #MeToo, but not recognized for the years of leadership she had put in, while Milano (and other famous white women alongside her) was heralded as a leader of the movement. When Burke said on Twitter that she wanted to be in service but that it stung to be acknowledged and erased, it cut me to the core. I had tasted that bitter fruit myself with consent culture.

While the discussion about sexual assault is an important one, another issue that is less recognized is of white people getting credit for Black people's labor. Reflecting on the entitlement present in that disconnect was, to me, also a vital part of the consent culture work I wanted to encourage. To me, credit, collaboration, and raising each other up was just as much consent culture as anything in the bedroom, but the mainstream had ignored that aspect. I was (and remain) determined to bring it back to the table.

I write this introduction in 2022. We are in a post-Trump world, but he left behind wreckage and trauma, as many abusers do. We are still in the middle of a global pandemic that has offered up many questions around bodily autonomy, what it means, and what we owe to each other. *Roe v. Wade* has been overturned, and with that decision, our rights to our own choices around reproduction have been reduced. Trans people are continually targeted by bigoted bills. I am looking toward being forty years old, and I feel like I am still uncovering more nuance when it comes to consent culture. I have spent half my life in the study of consent and power as an activist and as a person with lived experience, and I still feel humbled every day.

The feedback for *Ask* included that readers felt like a lot of good questions were raised but that there wasn't enough information on clear next steps. This was absolutely fair, and kind of what I intended—anyone who has been to one of my consent workshops will have experienced my stubborn refusal to claim that I have the solution to these issues. For me, being an anarchist activist means giving people the information to come to their own conclusions, finding ways to connect our conclusions, and creating coalitions.

I want to encourage people to think critically about their own lives and experiences, to think about where they could be choosing informed consent instead of our society's encouraged values of entitlement, disassociation, and pushing beyond your own limits. I can't possibly tell you how to do that. I have my own experiences and my own biases that color my response.

This Workbook

While I don't feel I can (or want to) give definitive solutions, I do think people can benefit from answering a lot of questions for themselves. I find it can help them come up with solutions and actions that fit their own lives and context. In keeping with my anarchist approach, I decided to write up the questions that I've asked myself and heard others ask over the years and put them together in the form of a workbook. The result is in your hands. Through twenty-eight prompts divided across four weeks, this workbook encourages you to explore your own assumptions, beliefs, and practices. Each exercise also includes a story from my own life or a contribution from another person who has experienced something relevant to that day's topic.

Week one is about you and your internal beliefs, week two is about your relationship to your loved ones, week three is about your relationship to your community, and week four reflects back on yourself and what you've discovered. While you could use sexual consent as a touchstone for many of the questions, the prompts are not meant to refer exclusively to sex or even to romantic relationships.

Please remember that you are allowed, even encouraged, to take your time working through this book—while it's formatted as a four-week program, you don't have to go at a particular pace, in any particular order, or to answer anything you don't want to. You might go through this in a month or a year. You may try to answer one question and then put the book under your bed for an indeterminate amount of time. I won't be offended, I promise! Taking care of yourself is key.

If I've done it right, this workbook may be hard work. You may find it thaws some survival dissociation or brings up trauma that has been dormant for years. Some prompts include revisiting a situation where you had to hear no, when you felt your boundaries had been crossed, or when you crossed someone else's. You may find yourself uncomfortable, defensive, or angry. All of these responses are absolutely understandable. We aren't often encouraged to do this kind of self-interrogation, and we're definitely not told to be kind to ourselves when we do. I hope that both the prompts and your own reactions to them are useful, whether you've only just started to explore what consent means to you or have years of experience as an activist or educator. I encourage you to take time to sit with yourself and clear your mind before reading the next entry.

While I initially envisioned this as a bunch of journaling prompts, it may also be a tool for a reading group to discuss or meditate on. It may be helpful to answer these questions with a therapist, with a small study group, or with a trusted partner. You may prefer to work through this on your own, or a mixture of alone and with others. Perhaps you take twenty minutes to write on these prompts, or an hour in discussion with friends. The space after each prompt may be enough for you, or you may want to fill a notebook with your thoughts. I hope that you can engage in a way that suits your needs.

This work can feel incredibly overwhelming, but we absolutely must address and abolish predatory power structures—racism, misogyny, homophobia, transphobia, ableism, fatphobia, ageism, classism, and more—to have the giving and receiving of pure consent. I also know that there's a lot of power to be had, both systematic and individual, in encouraging people to think critically, to explore, to experiment. I hope this book will help people with that process. While our everyday lives are embedded in those larger structures and imbued with their attendant problems, of course, we can each make change at a smaller and more personal scale, and that work ripples outward. The personal is political, as the saying goes!

The prompts and examples provided are meant to encourage you to think about your ideals as much, if not more, than your lived reality. This is about building a consent culture for yourself and your life. Other people will probably have different answers. Things that are consensual for you may be boundary violations for someone else, or vice versa. That is also absolutely OK—humans are not a monolith.

Consent culture (in my ideal form) is a living document, a scholarship that continues to adapt and evolve. I don't call myself a master of consent culture, because my responses grow with me and the people I encounter along the way. I think we all build off each other's work. For example, Planned Parenthood came up with an excellent acronym for assessing consent: FRIES (Freely given, Reversible, Informed, Enthusiastic, and Specific). Jenny Wilson, creator of the International Day of Consent and ConsentCulture.co.uk, prefers the word "engaged" over "enthusiastic," pointing out that you may not be enthusiastic about the act but are positive about the result. I found that this resonated a lot with me and have embraced it in my own educational materials.

It may feel intimidating that there isn't one right answer to these questions. It's scary to sit with the idea that we have probably crossed a boundary somewhere in our lives before, and we likely will again. But how exciting to be humble in that knowledge, to accept our fallibility and, instead of succumbing to despair and apathy, to want to strive to get as close to

100% consent as possible. How thrilling to seek to hurt each other (and ourselves) less!

For me, consent culture is less like a rigid foundation, staying in one place and crumbling when pushed, and more like a bridge—flexible yet secure, bringing people from our current lifetime toward a better future. Won't you join me on the other side?

WEEK ONE: INTROSPECTION

I find a lot of discussions about consent focus on the space between two people who want to be physically intimate. It's not a terrible place to focus on, especially as discussions around sexual assault still leave a lot to be desired. As a culture, we have a long way to go before we can say that we've mastered sexual consent.

That said, I want us to start this journey in a closer, deeper place—consent as it relates to ourselves. We have our own stories about when it is and isn't OK to consent, how one should give consent, when consent perhaps isn't necessary. We push ourselves past our own boundaries and sometimes that feels really good, but sometimes it feels really bad. More often than not, we disagree on what "consent" as a term actually means in practice.

How on earth could we hope to communicate our consent vulnerably and honestly and have it heard as we intended if we don't even agree on what consent means?

This week is focused on defining what consent means to you, personally. We'll explore what a consent culture might look like in our own minds. We'll think about what we hope to learn from this process and consider what lessons we may have picked up from our environment. We'll think about what lessons we can learn from people who don't share our perspective or demographic. Finally, we'll discover how to recognize when we're getting close to one of our boundaries and how to take care of ourselves in that moment.

I'm hoping that by starting with this introspective perspective, we'll create a firm foundation on which we can build our own understanding of consent culture, as both an ideal and as a lived practice.

Day One:
What Is Consent Culture?

One of the things I get asked for the most, as a consent educator and activist, is The Answer.

We all know that Rape Culture Is Bad, so therefore Consent Culture Must Be Good, right? Yes means yes and no means no, after all. Why is all of this so complicated? Why isn't there a formulaic solution for how to ascertain consent?

There are a lot of reasons why defining consent, what it impacts, and what it doesn't cover is ongoing and complex. For a start, cultural norms help to shape communication styles. For example, in some cultures, eating everything on your plate is a nonverbal signal that you are still hungry, while in other cultures if you don't eat everything on your plate, it means you didn't like the meal. No wonder people get their wires crossed!

Another thing that can add complexity to this conversation is individualism versus collectivism. In the United States, the idea of personal freedom is considered a core value by many Americans. In Japan, meanwhile, collectivism and knowing your role as part of a harmonious group is a core value. Both have some validity, and both have their shortcomings, especially when it comes to consent. While an American person may feel that protecting their personal ability to choose is more important than following the will of a group, a Japanese person may feel their fulfillment of their role as part of a community is more important than individual choice. Both people will likely define consent differently, as they each have a different lens through which they see the world.

Yet when we talk about consent, we often don't try to make sure that we're all talking about the same thing. It's difficult to be aware of your bias until you make a concerted effort to unpack it, but that's a vital aspect of this kind of work. Culture, upbringing, religion, ethnicity, politics, gender, physical and mental health—all of these add layers of understanding to a concept that is as amorphous as consent.

If we don't all have the same definition of consent, how could we possibly look for one easy answer that would work in all circumstances?

Most of the exercises in this workbook include one person telling a story from their experience, but for this first question it is useful to showcase two.

Yael R. Rosenstock Gonzalez, Puerto Rican Jewish pleasure activist and owner of SexPositiveYou, writes:

> If the culture of the world were to shift toward consent, we'd witness a dismantling of systems of oppression. When consent is at the center of how we interact, then accountability must also be, and this combination of values could change everything. But let me back up a bit from the utopia building in my head.
>
> When I think of consent culture, I envision people taking the well-being of others into account before acting. This translates to seeking to understand the needs and boundaries of those around us prior to fulfilling our own desires.
>
> In this physical sense, it means asking someone who is sad but doesn't love touch whether they want

a hug or a different form of comfort. Or asking those around you how they feel before you engage in something that might impact them, such as smoking nearby, choosing not to wear a mask in an enclosed space, or trying a new sexual act with them.

It would be more than that though—consent implies that we have all the information we need to make informed decisions. As a person who has seen many doctors in their life, consent for me would include full access to information regarding treatment options and side effects. It would look like letting a friend know that you are looking to emotionally dump on them and asking if they have the capacity to hold that. In workspaces, it would mean sharing salary information in the job posting and letting people know about job-related concerns before they start.

Consent also requires that there be options. If someone chooses to do something because they feel they have no other choice, it's coercion, not consent. Unfortunately, structural oppression denies people their right to sincere choice, whether that's feeling forced to go to work when you're sick, having to flat iron your hair to avoid losing your job, entering bathrooms that don't match your gender identity to avoid punishment, or needing to cross borders for your safety while being labeled a criminal.

True consent would also mean an upending of the US criminal justice system. We would have to re-evaluate the systemic issues that led to certain decisions (transformative justice), and we would need to speak with victims who were harmed to understand what they are seeking to restore balance (restorative justice).

Jenny Wilson, founder of ConsentCulture.co.uk and creator of the International Day of Consent, writes:

> Consent, for me, refers to agency and choice. If I am fully in consent (in accordance with the FRIES framework, spelled out in the glossary), then I am operating with full autonomy. In consent I'm using my agency to make choices that are free and unlimited by social or personal expectations, even subconscious ones.
>
> Consent culture would allow me to operate authentically, belonging instead of "fitting in." I want to be fully accountable for myself and the impact I make on the world and people around me. I believe consent lies at the heart of the idea that the personal is political (and vice versa). I think that if our interpersonal interactions were fully consensual, then the whole world would be much kinder and fairer than it is now.
>
> Consent operates in every connection we make, including:
> - How we give ourselves permission or tell ourselves what is and isn't OK.
> - Interpersonal relationships (e.g., from sex and intimacy to how we relate to a work colleague or a person living on the streets).
> - Group dynamics, peer pressure, and the different expectations of behaviour in a workplace or a social club.

- At the socio-cultural level, enshrined in law, retold in songs and stories, or absorbed by experiencing all the interactions around us.

It's difficult to imagine how consent culture would feel and how it would change the way we live because it would be a paradigm shift. The ways we behave, communicate, and think presently are constructed inside systems that lack consent. If we've spent our whole lives (as most of us have) operating inside a culture of entitlement, hierarchy, privilege, and coercion, it can be really difficult to notice the insidious ways our behaviours enable and perpetuate it.

I often tell myself I "must" do this or I "have to" do that. Perhaps I could instead ask myself if I "want to" or I'm "willing to." This subtle coercion turns up in interactions with others too. To my kid, I say "You have to get your shoes on." At work, we tell ourselves and others that "We must make the deadline." Out with friends, we say "You should keep this to yourselves."

Despite intentions, expressions like these reduce agency and choice. They hold assumptions about how much someone is willing or wanting to do something, and they demand or require a particular course of action. What is absent is curiosity, empathy, and an openness to hear "no."

Being able to say and hear "no" makes a "yes" way more yessy. Consent liberates us from expectations and assumptions. Consent culture requires intention, care, noticing, and communicating. Then the possibilities become endless.

We can try things, with no expectation to continue them. We can change our minds and opinions, with no assumption that we are open to new ideas. We can choose to cooperate because we want to make things happen together. We can celebrate our extraordinary differences, beyond the limits and assumptions of labels. We can take responsibility to learn and grow where our needs take us, to find light alongside each other.

Where are these definitions similar? Where do they differ? What do they focus on, and what do they leave out? All of this is useful data when we start this journey to better understand our relationship to consent, and what a consent culture could look like.

....

Prompt: What does the word "consent" mean to you? What about the idea of a "consent culture"? How would living in a consent culture change the way you interact with others? What could you apply "consent culture" as a concept to? How would it change how you treat your own boundaries? How would it influence how you deal with the world?

Day Two:
What Do You Want to Learn?

When I first started on this journey of exploring what consent actually, practically means, I had no idea how much it would impact my life. First of all, I figured I had a pretty good handle on it. I was raised by feminist parents who taught me a lot about sovereignty. I was fiercely independent and informed, and I started taking classes within the kink community when I was eighteen, so I was exposed early on in my adult life to concepts like "safe, sane, and consensual." I knew all the slogans: yes means yes, no means no, consent is sexy.

But as I began to do more research into the history of LGBTQ+ rights, I began to see some holes in all that feel-good, oversimplified phrasing. I learned that the age of consent for same-sex sexual activity was twenty-one in the UK, yet sixteen for heterosexual activity. I was sixteen when I found out that you couldn't legally consent to being spanked for fun thanks to a case in the news in Attleboro, Massachusetts. You couldn't legally consent to queer sex in the US until 2003, when *Lawrence v. Texas* ruled that criminal punishment for those who partake in anal sex was unconstitutional. I was nineteen at the time.

There are still complex laws in place that make "consent to harm" a gray area in many states, not just in the letter of the law but in the application. Laws intended to protect domestic violence victims end up being used against consensual kinky couples, while domestic violence victims who also explore BDSM can find their flogger collection cited as evidence that they are not, in fact, abused.

Zach Budd, Gulf Coast Area advocate for the National Coalition for Sexual Freedom, writes:

> I'm always interested in conversations about consent and the topic of consent. I am fascinated by the concepts of consent that people have, how they developed them, and where (or if) they were ever taught consent principles. Moreover, what informs the ideas that adults, to say nothing of children, hold about consent and what it means for activities to be "consensual"?
>
> When I educate myself, I am hoping to gain an understanding of consent in the past, the present, and the future.

I began to realize that the law was not the best arbitrator of what was actually consensual and what wasn't. But then, what was a more appropriate yardstick? What about when yes didn't mean yes, or when consent wasn't sexy? Whose job was it to make consent sexy? Was it anyone's job?

I didn't know, so I asked my friends. As we talked about our own experiences and how confusing it was to define what was and was not consensual (did we feel pressured to say yes? did we just... not say no?), I began to realize that there may not be a clear line in every situation.

I began to realize how often I had crossed a boundary because I didn't hear no, so that must mean yes, right? I began to realize how often I had ignored my own boundaries because I didn't feel confident enough to speak up for myself.

I began to realize how often I had felt too dissociated to say anything at all.

It was intense. And as I unpacked my feelings about my sexual experiences, I also began to realize when these situations had happened in other areas of my life. The dissociation at the dentist that made it hard for me to speak up when something hurt. The exhaustion from advocating for myself at the doctor's office that led to me minimizing my own chronic pain for twenty years. The social anxiety when I was in an unfamiliar space that often caused me to drink a little more than I should in order to cope.

I started to realize I didn't respect or even fully know what my own boundaries were, so how could I hope to communicate them to others?

As I realized that, I simultaneously realized how many times my boundaries had been crossed but I hadn't said anything about it because "it wasn't *that* bad." I was scared to assert my boundaries after the fact because I didn't want the trauma of instigating a callout revictimizing me, especially when I was pretty sure the other person didn't do it on purpose. Society really pushed this dynamic of "victim" and "abuser," but I didn't identify many of my experiences that way. Yet, I didn't want to minimize the situations that were abusive, either.

It didn't feel like there was a framework for centering consent in our interactions, just a fear imparted to us to avoid violation. I began to write about my process of exploring what it meant to move positively toward consent instead of simply protectively away from harm. Today, I'm still learning about the complex social dynamics that exist—how power dynamics subtly and explicitly impact someone's ability to withdraw or give consent, how to hold people accountable while letting them be fallible, and when to assess someone as too dangerous for that grace.

I decided to make this workbook in part because I had all these questions for myself, and I realized that considering them was a deeply healing and transformative process for me. I hope you will find it so as well.

Prompt: Exploring our relationship to consent is a long, complicated, and sometimes emotionally fraught process. What made you want to pick up this book? What are you hoping to learn?

WEEK ONE: INTROSPECTION

Day Three:
When Should You Take a Break
From This Personal Work?

It can be difficult to figure out how to have healthy boundaries, period. It's even harder when you're a go-to person to help people with triggering issues like consent violations, addiction, domestic violence, suicidality, etc. It can feel impossible to set a boundary, even for your own well-being. The work is vital and necessary, yes, but you aren't an automaton!

My personal experience:

> I never intended to become a consent culture activist. I mean, I cared about consent, but I always figured it would be just one aspect of other types of activism I did, because I assumed that all people had the same definition of consent and that they all saw "consent culture" in the same way I did. The more I talked to my friends, the more I began to realize how wrong I was, and how overwhelming being a face of this kind of work was going to be. I fell into being an activist, but I forgot to be a person too.
>
> In 2011, fresh to consent culture activism, I set up the Safe/Ward Blog Carnival, where people all across the internet would write about consent culture during a certain week and then we'd all link to

each other's pieces. In addition, because I knew that the topic was a scary one to discuss under your own name, I offered people the ability to send me their own stories for me to post anonymously. I expected to get maybe twenty or so stories.

I got hundreds of (often graphic and detailed) stories of abuse, often with desperate pleas for solutions on how to handle them. For months. It was so overwhelming that my collaborator immediately quit the project, leaving me to figure out what to do with this wasp's nest I had just smacked out of a tree. At the time I was twenty-seven and just coming to terms with my own assaults within the BDSM community. I was starting to realize how many traumatizing situations I had told myself were normal because I needed to believe that in order to keep myself from falling apart.

It was so bad that it impacted my personal life in a myriad of ways. I found myself increasingly using substances to cope while withdrawing emotionally and sexually from my partners, my anxiety increasing every time I opened my email. At the same time, I didn't feel like I could walk away because the people who were coming to me were people who didn't feel safe anywhere else, and they were telling me deeply personal stories. It felt disrespectful to not respond.

I ended up withdrawing from sex education for a few years and left the sex-positive community almost entirely. I felt bitter that consent projects focusing on quips flirtily spoken by hot porn stars were embraced by my communities while my work had been publicly at best patronized and at worst ostracized. While individuals privately thanked me for my willingness to stand up and say something, I had very little outward-facing support. Meanwhile, people were still being violated by "community leaders" with no accountability. I felt completely and utterly burned out.

After 2012, I gave myself a few years to take a break from this kind of work. Instead, I went to therapy and got in touch with my own needs and wants. I was able to return to consent culture work feeling refreshed, with a better understanding of my boundaries. I was able to publish *Ask: Building Consent Culture* after that period of rest. I decided to prioritize sustainability in how I approached activism. I made sure I went to bed at a reasonable hour, set up office hours for myself, and figured out ways for the community to proactively compensate me for the work I did for those who needed me. Now when I feel my chest tightening or I feel a sense of dread while opening my email, I have people I can decompress with. I take walks, I cook myself a filling meal—I take a break *before* I feel drained. And when I feel especially indulgent? I turn off my phone entirely.

I often remind people to put on their own oxygen masks first so they can assist others. I find that people close to burnout end up barely being able to put their own mask on at all, and you can't help others when you're gasping for air. By doing a little maintenance and making sure you don't get to that edge, you can find a steady but stable way to do even difficult work on yourself and your communities.

Compassion fatigue is real. Emotional burnout is real. It's better to take a moment to care for yourself today and tomorrow and the day after than to help everyone else in the plane and then not do anything for anyone ever again. Allow yourself space to step away so you aren't scared to step up again.

....

Prompt: Sometimes discussions about intense topics can be triggering, bringing up situations in the past where we felt helpless, confused, alone, or something else rough. Do you have triggers (physical and emotional responses to a disturbing topic)? What red flags (physical and emotional signs that you are experiencing post-traumatic stress) do you see that let you know when a situation is getting to be too intense? How do you care for yourself in those moments and de-escalate yourself? When and how do you give yourself permission to take a break from the work of introspection and public activism?

DAY THREE: WHEN SHOULD YOU TAKE A BREAK?

Day Four:
What Are Your Boundaries?

As a society, we focus a lot on one individual crossing another individual's boundaries as the gold standard for demonstrating what consent is and is not. It's not a bad place to start—we clearly have enough issues defining consent when it's externally expressed between two entities, so why make it more complicated than that? Don't run before you can walk.

However, I notice that a lot of situations in which I'm asked for my expertise involve more ambiguity. Sometimes in the situations I'm asked to mediate, it sounds like permission was granted and then, when that thing was happening, those boundaries changed internally for one of the participants but they found it hard to vocalize this. Defining the difference between a hard boundary (no, not under any circumstance) and a soft boundary (not right now, but maybe under the right conditions) can be complex even when we're just defining it for ourselves.

Intimacy ConAmore, polyamorous advocate and sexuality educator, writes:

> One of my boundaries I've had a lot of experience asserting and defining: no anal play. Some people take this as an assumption that I simply haven't tried it and don't know what I am missing. Often,

they try to coerce me into it, under the guise of "it's the best orgasm you'll ever have."

Don't get me wrong—I have tried it and enjoyed it immensely. I miss being able to have anal sex now that I literally can't. But I have permanent damage from physical birthing scars. Also, I don't have to justify any of my boundaries in response to some other person's inquiries.

In the past, I would talk myself into giving in to someone else's desires despite my own body or mind having other objections to it. I've tried to do anal rehab so I could enjoy it again. I pushed my boundaries, trying to work past the pain and focus on the pleasure, but the pain was far too great. Pain is not a pleasure for me the way it can be for others. It kills my vibe and makes me feel disconnected from pleasure. It's just not happening. I know my body.

Sometimes I miss and think about the pleasure my body has previously experienced with anal play. When you miss something so pleasurable, there's this pressure to make every effort trying to have success experiencing things that your body and mind crave. And honestly, some of these times, I felt empowered about trying to extend the growth of my comfort zone for certain experiences.

Even so, too many times in my past I felt like I betrayed myself. I asked myself why I didn't stick to my "no" or to my boundary. So now, I don't compromise myself unless I am enthusiastically wanting to change a boundary of my own volition—not because of someone else's desires for me to do so.

It's not always just boundaries shifting toward a no, either. I'm thinking of a time where I was freshly doing consent culture advocacy and was pretty raw. A woman I was flirting with after a workshop came outside with me to continue our conversation. Eventually, mid-banter, I asked her if I could kiss her—I assumed a no unless I received a yes. She pulled away from me with a look of mild disgust and said, "um, obviously—but it kind of ruins the magic when you ask," adding that I should have just done it in the moment. I was kind of surprised, since we had just been talking about how important it was to make negotiations clear before doing anything. The boundaries had changed for her in relation to me—I just hadn't been updated!

It made me think a lot about times that I said one thing but found myself wishing, in my heart, for something different. It also made me think about the times I had broken my own soft boundaries. One time I agreed to go on a hike and found myself not enjoying it anymore (feeling my knee in some pain), yet I pushed myself to keep going because I didn't want to disappoint the other person or admit to my injury. I wondered how many times a boundary violation was a little hopeful thinking from one person intermingling with reluctance to speak up on the part of the other person.

How often do we violate our own internal boundaries to not make a fuss?

....

Prompt: List out some hard and soft boundaries that you've set for yourself. Are there external circumstances under which you may waver on these boundaries? Can you think of any times that you've pushed or challenged your own boundaries? What were your reasons? How did you feel afterward?

Day Five:
What Are Your Advantages
and Challenges?

While I may be accused by some of being "the PC police" for encouraging people to reflect on the various advantages they may be granted in their day-to-day lives, and in which ways they may be marginalized, I think it's a valuable exercise.

We all exist in complex dynamics with each other, where race, class, gender, sexual orientation, citizenship, physique, and mental health all commingle to create a tangled mess of who has power and when. Institutional oppression exists and impacts the populace in a variety of ways—the police pull over more Black folks than white folks, for example, and female athletes get less money and fewer sponsorship opportunities than their male counterparts.

We are products of our environment and upbringing, which impacts our outlook on our position in the world. Growing up in the suburbs, I was weirdly, inexplicably anxious around houseless people when I moved to the city, until I started to spend time talking to them and humanizing them. I have a friend who was "allowed" by his family to date whomever he wanted, as long as he married a nice Jewish girl. How might that cultural expectation impact his behavior with others? It's an interesting thing to unpack.

Kori Doty, genderqueer community educator and host of the podcast *Imagination Revolution: UBI,* writes:

Before I started pursuing medical transition, I had a number of experiences with trans masculinity that had adopted trappings of conventional, toxic masculinity. Looking back, I can see the motivation for these men to find security in their gender by replicating the attitudes and behaviours of cis men as a mechanism to achieve safety and gender affirmation, but also as a means of occupying a more advantaged position in a sexist society. As a young genderqueer, seeing this approach to adopting masculinity, I was disgusted and even distanced myself from the possibility that I was trans masc, as I didn't want to transition into that sort of asshole. When I did reach the point that I realized that I did need to pursue hormones and eventually surgeries, I did so with an intentional caution and personal commitment to using the power I may gain access to in good ways.

As I started being read in the world more consistently as a white man, I found that sometimes the ways that I was privileged were invisible to me, even with that intent.

I had partners who were women and queers of colour and size who tried to help me see the pieces that my whiteness, thin body, middle-class upbringing, and relative able-bodiedness kept me from being aware of. Sometimes I heard it, and other times fragility and defensiveness prevented me from being able to actually hear and integrate their generous shares in good ways. My fear and fragility kept me from being fully able to own some of the ways that I had more social capital than those I was in relationship with. I saw the parallels of transness, queerness, and survivor experiences and used them to invalidate and ignore the issues of race, size, ableism, and misogyny that I had gotten a pass on. Looking back, I can see more clearly why these friends and lovers became so exasperated in their attempts to get me onside to allyship. I was inadvertently doing a version of the same thing I had hated and committed to not doing, while telling myself that I wasn't and couldn't.

Now in my thirties, I am sure I still have holes in my compassion perspectives but I am more open to admitting that and try to be less reactive about having them pointed out. I know that I can walk into male-dominated spaces and be instantly given more assumed credit than a femme-presenting counterpart, even if/when she is more knowledgeable than me. I know that I do not face the same level of threat of physical violence as many others, as I am now read as a tall, moustached, leather-clad, middle-aged white guy. I can take myself for a walk through a "rough" neighborhood in the middle of the night, and as much as I was socialized to walk with my keys between my knuckles, I don't anymore. I try to move through public space with the awareness that I am more likely to be read as predator than prey. I still try to use my power and access for good when I can, but a big piece of that, and one that has made more sense over time, is the power in humility.

Toxic masculinity and white supremacy are built around the idea of invulnerable experts; that power never admits it's not earned but occupies an assumed arrogance. To truly come into relating well to my adopted power, I had to come to place where

I could own that my being read as white, my being
read as male, my being read as able-bodied (while
not entirely accurate) do still give me advantage
and that a part of how those advantages operate is
by keeping me from seeing and understanding the
experiences of folks who aren't read in these ways.
Admitting that privilege creates gaps in perspective
and knowledge is a needed balancing element. The
more access and social capital we may have access
to, the more places we may need to practice humility, compassionate decentering, and deep listening.

As individuals, sometimes we leverage our power on the side
of good (for example, perhaps we make more money due at
least in part to that advantage, so we send donations to folks
who are struggling), and sometimes we abuse it to get what
we want (an employer telling an employee to stay late, even
though they won't be paid extra for their labor). This will of
course impact the situations in which we feel comfortable
saying no to someone, and those in which we don't, even if
we want to. This reminds me that other people feel intimi-
dated by me, and that I need to make an effort to reduce that
as much as I can while still understanding where it exists and
where it comes from.

Having a better understanding of the ways in which I wield
power over others, consciously or subconsciously, helps me
be more mindful of how I'm doing it. And understanding how
precarious my advantages can be causes me to want to use
them to their utmost potential, not just for me, but to raise
everyone up with me.

Prompt: What sort of social advantages do you think you have? In what ways might you be marginalized? How might that influence your relationship to your ability to say yes or to say no? Is there a time you adopted a boundary from your family or friends because of cultural expectations? What was this experience like? How did those pressures complicate your own boundaries?

Day Six:
How Can You Expand
Your Scope?

It can be difficult to notice the ways in which we have become set in our ways. We are all the products of our upbringing, our environment, how society sees us, and how we see ourselves. All of these things combine to give us a perception of how the world works, and our place in it. This can be a good thing in some ways, as that perception can solidify our sense of self and make us feel secure in our identity. It can also be limiting if we only encounter and experience the perspectives of people similar to ourselves. It can be harder to truly have compassion for others when we have no sense of who they are.

A little story from my past:

> When I was in my teens and twenties, I was absolutely 100% a riot grrl to the core. I read all the feminist zines and books I could get my hands on, from the dreamy queer fantasy of Francesca Lea Block to the fury against fatphobia from Marilyn Wann. I devoured *Dykes to Watch Out For* and especially enjoyed sex-positive feminist writing like that from Susie Bright, Carol Queen, and Dossie Easton. I considered myself well-read, my perspective wide.
>
> It took me an embarrassingly long time to recognize that while the subjects I read about were varied,

almost everything I read was by white women from liberal cities like myself. I hadn't done that intentionally, but I certainly seemed to be drawn to voices that were similar to my own. While there were certainly things to learn there, I wasn't really challenging my beliefs or examining them from another angle.

From there, I started to make an effort to read Black feminist theory, writing from queer activists around the world, and memoirs by Indigenous writers. I began to form a more holistic understanding of my thoughts on consent and power and love and intimacy, not just based on reflections of my own lived experiences but informed by the diversity and complexity of people's lives that were very different from mine. I hadn't realized how US-centric a lot of my understanding of feminism was.

I also made a point of going back and reading feminist theory from before my time. I read Andrea Dworkin. I read Gloria Steinem. I read Catherine McKinnon. These were feminist writers I had been dismissive of because we parted ways significantly on some issues close to my heart, like sex work or trans issues. I still believe their perspectives on these topics were wrong, but I am now better able to make a strong argument against them because I have more perspective. And, more interestingly, there were snippets that I found myself agreeing with so much they became part of how I teach consent culture. The idea that 100% consent isn't really possible under a white supremacist capitalist patriarchy is one that is informed (at least in part) by second-wave feminism.

Expanding my scope gave me context for where we are now by showing me where we came from. It also demonstrated to me how important it is to give credit where credit is due.

While I was working on this question, a movie came out that had at its center a teenage Chinese-Canadian girl. Several reviewers spoke disparagingly about how it wasn't a universal story and the perspective it was showcasing was too narrow to reach widespread audiences. I found that a fascinating thing to say. I grew up watching plenty of movies about what it was like to be a white teenage straight boy in the 1980s, and I was a white queer teen in the late 1990s, yet I was able to find aspects of those films relatable. Awkwardness and rebellion are pretty universal teen experiences, even if we manifest them differently.

It is important to expose ourselves to perspectives that are unlike our own, in part to demonstrate to us how many feelings and situations are pretty universally human, even if the details differ, and in part to give us some insight into cultural differences. I don't have to see myself perfectly reflected in an essay or a video to gain something from it. After all, the only thing I have in common with the lead of *It's a Wonderful Life* is having felt wild despair, but I still find it a moving story.

....

Prompt: Much of the conversation on consent in the mainstream media has been dominated by cisgender white women (like me!). Receiving other perspectives on a topic can bring about a more nuanced understanding of the subject. I invite you to read writing on consent, accountability, and justice by someone who is not of the same ethnicity, culture, and/or gender identity as you, and write at least a paragraph on what you learned and what resonated with your own experiences. There's a list of resources in the back of this book to get you started. Even if you already make an effort to consider other perspectives, maybe this exercise will help you discover someone new.

WEEK ONE: INTROSPECTION

Day Seven: What Stories Have You Internalized?

There are so many ways in which unspoken expectations become rooted in us through repeated representation in the media and reflection in our day-to-day lives. One such story that really impacted me was the idea that for consent to be valid, it needed to be enthusiastic—a "fuck yes." Early on in my consent activism, I really appreciated the idea of "yes means yes" going around colleges. The focus was on getting and giving a clear affirmative instead of waiting to hear dissent.

While it was useful for me to reflect on whether my yes was a "fuck yes" or an "eh, OK," I also began to realize that consent could still be valid even if it was unenthusiastic. The story that consent was only "real" if it was wholeheartedly positive was not one that served me.

Jenny Wilson, founder of ConsentCulture.co.uk and creator of the International Day of Consent, writes:

> It's a tale as old as time. True love. Once you find it, you'll live happily ever after.
>
> I've been told and sold that story over and over, as a child and since. It's in most fairy tales, songs, and movies. It set me off in search of a rare and scarce version of love, a love to be treasured and defended, a love so magical it would triumph over

all. It sounded like the most important quest in my life, so I invested quite a lot of time and energy into finding it.

As I searched, if I met someone who might be that person, I became pretty fixated on them and on finding out if this was true love. If it wasn't, I'd drop that whole relationship, and all the possibilities that went with it. Friendship? Not as important. An intellectual spark to work together? No, too complicated, and definitely not with an ex.

This story comes with a library of subplots. We know them so well they form our assumption that we're "on the same page" of our relationship. Try Googling "when to say I love you"—pages of results tell you to wait for ten dates, or three months, or some other relationship "milestone." These stories and assumptions are both gendered and binary—female characters rescued by male heroes, unsuspecting bachelors trapped by desperate spinsters.

Assumptions aren't consent. Assumptions can override intentional choices, decisions, and thoughtfulness about how we want to engage in loving relationships. There's a script to follow: start casual, get serious, go steady, become exclusive, move in together, entwine finances, co-parent, marry, or whatever comes next in the well-worn path of true love. Some of these assumptions are dangerous. If love is rare and conquers all, it becomes hard to leave a relationship that might be love, even if that relationship is hurting you. No relationship is more important than the people in it. The script for breakups has us all taking sides. What if you never find another, better love? What if you're left on the bookshelf, alone?

Once I threw away the script, I realised the reality that love is abundant. Humans are wired for connection, and we seek and form all kinds of loving connections throughout our lives. Learning to love yourself enables you to recognise and ask for what you want and need, and to ask those that you love to communicate their wants and needs. By loving with openness, in full consent, we can figure out what works for us in any given situation. Connections can shift and change around us and the many people we love as we journey through our lives.

I love people I'd describe as my family, friends, lovers, colleagues, community—in some cases, people who fit several of those descriptors. And I love them without limiting them or myself inside a story that none of us consented to be part of. True love is a story you write for yourself.

One of the ways I personally learned to love myself better was delving more deeply into the stories I have internalized, trying to understand what impact they might have. As a sex worker, sometimes I said "fuck yes" to paying my bills, even if I said "eh, OK" to the sexual desires of the client. I bristled at the idea from some feminists that I had to love my job at all times or I was being coerced and objectified. No one ever insisted I have enthusiastic consent when I was working in the mall! When my dentist asked me to come in at 8 a.m. to finish my root canal, I agreed, even though I hate being up early and hate going to the dentist. The end result was something I wanted, so I said yes. But I wasn't enthusiastic about it!

This exploration gave me a much more nuanced and complicated understanding of consent and made me think a lot about why the story of "yes means yes" was so important to me. I wanted the security of clarity, the safety of not feeling differently about a situation later. But even an enthusiastic yes in the moment can feel differently down the line with more context. Accepting that was important for me in understanding some of my own difficult experiences.

....

Prompt: We all live in a culture of stories that influence how we interpret the world. Examples include the value of bootstrapping, what makes a successful relationship, and what makes a person beautiful. What are some of the stories that impact your understanding of consent? How do these stories serve you? How do they hold you back? Have those stories changed as you've gotten older? Do you interpret the stories differently in some way?

WEEK TWO:
OUR RELATIONSHIP
TO EACH OTHER

Understanding and contextualizing our own experiences with consent is an important foundation for creating a consent culture lens.

Now, let's take another step forward—this time into the space between us and another. In this week, we'll explore consent when it brushes up against someone else. That could be a romantic or sexual partner, a friend, a family member, or someone else close to us. After all, many of our first experiences thinking about consent more seriously occur when we're reflecting on an interaction between us and someone we know.

As I said in week one, I've found many articles and books that talk extensively about consent between lovers, and, realistically, that's not a bad thing to focus on. Unfortunately, when so much discussion around the topic is only from the perspective of sexual and romantic partners, it can muddle the fact that these discussions are equally vital for other close relationships in our lives, like our friends and family. Saying no to a lover and saying no to a family member can be difficult in similar, socially entrenched ways. We are fed a lot of stories about how one should never say no to someone one loves, after all, whether that be "because they're family" or "because they're your partner." Yet when the language is so focused on conversations around sex and romance, it can be difficult to untangle the advice from the context.

In the week ahead, we'll explore what we like to give to others, and what we like to receive. We'll think about the word "no" and what about it feels difficult to say and to hear, and we'll look at a few different ways to reframe our understanding. We'll touch on intimacy and consent, both sexual and not, to consider how we can make discussions about it playful as well as effective.

Day Eight:
What Are Your Limits?

Limits are an interesting thing to think about. We are often encouraged to push our limits, like in exercise, to make ourselves slightly uncomfortable, to "go past our comfort zone." It is seen as a positive thing, a successful thing, to define something as a limit, and then move past it. Physical therapy however has taught me that there is a difference between challenging yourself and causing yourself more injury. The line between the two can be pretty gray and hard to identify, but whew, when I cross it and am nursing a sprain for a week, it can be pretty frustrating!

Here's a little more background into my experience with this:

> I identified as a people pleaser for most of my life. When I was younger, I internalized the story that relationships were work, which isn't a bad story on its own. After all, it's important to be willing to make an effort for the people and things we care about, right?
>
> The problem was that I often pushed myself too hard in my desire to "do the work" and please my partner. I was so focused on what my partner wanted, and my desire to provide that for them, that I didn't have any idea what *I* wanted. I only knew

that I felt resentful and dissatisfied. I figured that this must mean I needed to work harder and give even more. And thus, I became more resentful and frustrated, and that would trickle out onto my partners, who often had no idea I was putting myself through this.

By not being honest about my limits with myself, never mind my partners, I wove myself into a web of manipulation in order to avoid conflict. I thought that I could just work on myself and I would eventually get over my feelings. It took many years to realize that I was actually resentful of myself and how trapped I had made myself feel in my attempts to people-please my way into safety. What had happened instead was a situation where no one involved was able to give informed consent, because none of us had all the information.

It feels remarkable that I can now feel totally comfortable leaving a situation that doesn't serve me. I used to feel terrified of breakups, whether with friends or lovers, and I would do almost any amount of contorting to avoid them. Now, however, I understand my limits. I know what I am flexible about, and what I'm not. I know how to ask for what I want and need, and when I give something, I can give it freely.

Everyone has a slightly different framework for how they talk about relationships, consent, and boundaries. For example, the book *The Art of Receiving and Giving: The Wheel of Consent* by Betty Martin offers one such framework, beginning with lessons from early childhood but spanning out to any and all interactions in our day-to-day lives.

Now, her framework is complex enough that it really does take a whole book to get into the intricacies, but I'll summarize as best I can. She breaks consent down into four quadrants: you do what you want (taking quadrant), you do what they want (serving quadrant), they do what you want (accepting quadrant), and they do what they want (allowing quadrant). Martin gives examples of how each of these quadrants is related to your consent, the other person's, and the relationship's own dynamics. To be aware of which quadrants are in play is to be actively in touch with yourself and your desires at any given time.

One example given in the book mentions Amy, who asked for her back to be massaged. Brent stepped up and rubbed her shoulders for three minutes, both people seeming happy and satisfied. Afterward, Amy said that she enjoyed it for the first minute but spent the next two minutes wondering how to ask Brent to go a little lighter. She went from being within the accepting quadrant to being in the allowing quadrant, from what she wanted to what she didn't mind. Understanding that shift might help Amy speak up sooner and might also help Brent understand that the same action (the massage) may be received differently at different moments. The hope is that understanding this will help them communicate more effectively in the future.

This can be one useful way to determine what dynamics are enjoyable for you and can also help you assess how you feel about an offering so that you can better define your limits. Martin encourages us to do some fundamental work into noticing what we want, into knowing our boundaries, and into communicating them.

We live in a culture that is made up of contradictions. We are encouraged to value freedom and independence, but also told not to make a fuss and to let things go to keep the peace. While we tell each other that it's important to speak up when we're harmed, we also live in a society where doing so can have consequences that can last years. It can be difficult to determine how to establish our boundaries when we're encouraged to ignore them in order to please those around us. I appreciate the examples and proposed exercises in *The Art of Receiving and Giving*, which are one helpful way to look at our limits from a variety of perspectives.

I hope that you find this workbook another useful tool in exploring these dynamics.

....

Prompt: Martin says that "the way to joy and generosity is not to push ourselves, but to own our limits." What is your relationship to your limits with loved ones? Have you found yourself trying to like or do something in order to please another? Have you realized that someone is doing something to please you? What impact did that have on your life and your feelings?

....
....
....
....
....
....
....
....
....
....
....
....

Day Nine:
What Do You Like to Offer?

I've noticed a lot of my activism has been moving away from relating to the world by means of what to avoid. I used to define myself by what I was against, identifying problems and then placing myself and my work in contrast to that. I still do, to some extent. I identify as an antifascist, for example, and I focus a lot of my work around how it seeks to dismantle authoritarian ideals as I see them.

There's something to be said for spelling out what we are against as a starting place for guidelines and community building, but it's sometimes harder and more important to say what we're for.

Leslee Petersen, activist for LGBTQ+/polyamorous rights and ex-libertarian, writes:

> I enjoy offering my home to others when needed. I do this by hosting regular get-togethers for local friend groups and communities I am a part of. I frequently offer my home when events are being discussed. My friend group is composed of many people in apartments or shared living spaces. I have the privilege of having housing that allows me to accommodate larger groups for events and a yard for socializing. I share my home with only my spouse and pets, making planning easy.

I also make it known to my friends that my house is a safe space to go to when in need. I have been a space for grief, for crisis, for respite. My home is always open, with tea and cookies and a listening empathetic ear. I make and send food if they express it will be helpful. I open my couch and spare bed. My community and friends know that I and my home are open to them because I am not shy about making it known to them. If I hear from someone close that they are overwhelmed or near crisis, I reach out gently.

I live with disability and opening my home and being a safe space for my friends is a way I can give to my community without undue stress on my body. I feel valued as part of my friend group and community when my offers are appreciated, and I know my offering is appreciated whether or not they take me up on it at the moment. I feel valued, and I feel as if I am offering something of value. It's easy to view what we do for others as purely for their sake, but the feeling we get from giving to our communities should not be disregarded—there's great value in feeling pride in giving and offering to others.

Trying to narrow down what I was striving toward is what started consent culture as a concept in the first place. I was looking to define what kind of relationship I wanted to encourage as a building block for activism instead of focusing on the thing I wanted to discourage.

While this is true on a bigger scale for, say, political platforms (it's not enough to say you're anti-racist—you have to demonstrate what you *do* in solidarity), it's also true in interpersonal relationships. I know my friends have asked me out to eat before and I've listed off all the foods I didn't want to eat before they gently interrupted and said "OK, we know what you don't want, but what do you want?"

What do I want? Not just what do I want to receive, but what do I want to offer? I think it's difficult to answer because I don't always know. What I want changes from hour to hour, day to day, year to year. Twenty years ago I was a goth who spent most of her time at nightclubs. Now I dress in cardigans and go to bed by 11 p.m. after watching *Murder, She Wrote*. What I want isn't a stagnant thing. Often what I don't want feels more stable and consistent. Sometimes I am comfortable negotiating (e.g., I want to watch something under an hour long before bed, and I'd like it to be relatively light, but it doesn't have to be *Murder, She Wrote*) and sometimes I really want something in particular. It's taken a while to figure out when I feel OK being flexible and when it really means something to me, and even longer to learn how to communicate it.

For many of us, our wants are hard to define, and perhaps this speaks to how little practice we get talking about them. I've realized there are a few things that give me a lot of pleasure to offer to others, such as networking connections or cooking a meal for someone I care about. These things make me feel fulfilled, rather than drained, and when someone receives them gratefully, I feel cared about and seen. I've begun to reflect on how I feel when I offer various services to other folks, and I'm beginning to understand better under what conditions I feel empowered to share my time and space. By knowing that, it's made my boundaries even more stark, while also offering me a way to negotiate when appropriate.

Prompt: We often talk about what we say no to and what our boundaries are. But instead of defining ourselves by what we dislike, let's consider what we say yes to and what we like. What do you like doing? What do you enjoy offering to others? How do you offer it? How do you feel when your offering is welcomed? When do you believe negotiation is appropriate, and who should bring it up? Under what circumstances do you feel these things may shift?

Day Ten:
What Do You Like to Receive?

I've had a lot of therapists encourage me to think about what I want from other people. I've always found this a struggle to define, as I felt like I often wanted many things, and they changed all the time. Sometimes the things I wanted seemed to counter each other, like wanting to have time to focus on my hobbies but also needing time with people to feel cared about. It was easier to think about what I could give, and then I just... got what I got. That sometimes led to resentment—of myself, of the other person, of the situation. It wasn't ideal.

Intimacy ConAmore, polyamorous advocate and sexuality educator, writes,

> There are a lot of things I like to receive in my close relationships, including cuddles, platonic showers together, or nap dates. There's something especially wonderful about sharing nonsexual touch time. It's soothing. It's building intimacy unrelated to sex.
>
> I keep things pretty simple—I just tell my people that these are my favorite things to do with people I'm close to! Knowing what I like makes asking for it directly a lot easier. And having practice doing it and being heard has made me feel even more confident about sharing what my desires and needs are.

> Asking for what I want is one of my main forms of
> self-care. Closed mouths don't get fed.

We can learn new ways to communicate our desires from a lot of different places. For me, Gary Chapman's book *The Five Love Languages* was instrumental in helping me understand what sort of bids for connection I liked to receive. It gave me the language to recognize that quality time made me feel loved, while I could do without physical touch. Even though it was written from a very heteronormative, marriage-focused, Christian point of view, it still gave me a good starting place for identifying what behaviors made me feel loved and how I expressed that love to others.

Still, five love languages didn't feel like enough to me. It was a good starting place, but it was also clearly focused on romantic and sexual relationships. What about the ways I needed to feel loved by my friends and my community?

Anne Hodder-Shipp filled that gap for me with her book *Speaking from the Heart: 18 Languages for Modern Love*, which offered up a wider understanding of expressing affection and care. She included things like active listening and solidarity as ways one could express care in relationships, not just romantic, but also friendships and family. It made me realize that mutual accountability was an important way I felt held by my community, which is part of why I'm so devoted to consent culture.

It also helped me understand why I enjoyed receiving what I do. I spend a lot of time and energy on community leadership and guidance, so things that involve someone investing that kind of time and energy into me feel really special. While gifts are nice, they don't feel as emotionally fulfilling as scheduled time where we can share an experience together. Knowing that has helped me communicate my wants with others and better understand what they want. Feeling seen in that moment of vulnerability fills me with acknowledgment that's better for me than any physical touch.

....

Prompt: What are some things you enjoy receiving? What makes those things enjoyable for you? How do you ask for them? How do you feel when you ask for what you want?

Day Eleven:
How Do You Hear "No"?

I've noticed a strange paradox in my years doing consent culture work. I was brought up in the United States, where hearing "no" is often seen as just an opportunity to charm/cajole someone into saying "yes." Hell, I once saw a motivational poster in an office that said "every no gets you closer to yes." This may feel inspiring when it comes to creative ideas but is deeply alarming when it comes to interpersonal relationships.

Sunny Megatron, XBIZ Sex Educator of the Year 2021 and cohost of *American Sex Podcast*, writes:

> As both a consent educator and lifelong student, I've long felt that we don't talk enough about understanding and processing rejection. Emotions around boundary setting get the most airtime in consent education—and for good reason. We collectively acknowledge the immense amount of self-work involved in learning to set healthy limits and resisting harmful patterns.
>
> Consent-savvy folks know how important it is for initiators to empower their partners in consent decisions. After all, reinforcing someone's "no" by responding with "thank you for taking care of yourself" is consent 101. But what about the unpleasant

emotions so many of us experience when we receive that "no"?

When I'm navigating consent, I default to the standard logic-based response to rejection. It's also what I teach: "If someone says 'no,' respect it, period. Don't ask why, don't push, don't coerce. Accept it while acknowledging that being firm in their limits may have been challenging for the boundary setter and move on." But, just like you, I'm also human. And sometimes when I least expect it, that "no" secretly lands like a gut punch.

Rejection can trigger deep insecurities that fool us into believing we're fundamentally flawed at our core. We may feel disappointed, judged, like we're too much, not enough, embarrassed, broken, as if we don't belong or we're undeserving of love.

Each time this happens to me, even though I respond how I'm logically supposed to, those unfavorable emotions still sometimes take me by surprise. Of course, I keep this to myself because I don't want to deprioritize my partner's self-care. That's when the shame sets in. Why, despite empowering my partners in their yeses and nos, do I feel crummy sometimes when I hear that empowered "no"? Does that mean I'm selfish? Am I doing precisely what consent education tells us never to do? Am I making my partner's self-advocacy about me?

Consent education sometimes glosses over the very real and valid emotions that can accompany rejection with the spirit of "suck it up, buttercup." In the past, I've internalized this message as, "feeling emotions in response to rejection is wrong." Nothing could be further from the truth, however. We can't necessarily control the emotions that creep up inside us. What is ours to control is our behavior in response to them.

When we're not prepared for these feelings (meaning, we haven't devised a strategy for recognizing and working through them in real time), our knee-jerk reaction may be to defuse them by any means necessary. We ignore the discomfort, hoping it will go away. Instead, it may fester under the surface and force itself out at inopportune times or in damaging ways. Sometimes we become angry, lash out, respond passive-aggressively, disengage, or coerce our partners.

A light-bulb realization for me was recognizing that the pain that accompanies rejection (including perceived rejection or fear of rejection) is valid and nothing to be ashamed of. Equally as important is recognizing that I am responsible for managing those emotions. I cannot rely on shifting that responsibility to my partners. Why? Expecting our partners to quell our feelings of disappointment can negatively impact their autonomy and disempower them in their consent decisions. Existing power imbalances can further magnify this.

Doing the self-work to build rejection resiliency can be a lengthy and difficult process. I also believe it's a vital component in creating consent culture and something every one of us can benefit from working on. Learning to process rejection looks different for everyone. It's up to you to customize a framework that resonates with you. Just as developing the skills for healthy boundary setting is often a complicated process, learning to manage rejection can be too. So be easy on yourself.

You would think in a culture that tells us that no is just a stepping stone to yes, people would shrug off hearing the word "no." After all, it's just a step on the path, right? Yet fear of rejection keeps people from asking for help, inviting people they like on dates, asking for a raise, or otherwise putting themselves out there. We are often so scared to hear the word "no" that we will hurt ourselves struggling to avoid even the potential of it. Why the dissonance?

There are a lot of interesting theories about why we are so avoidant of rejection. Maybe we're hardwired to be nervous if we don't feel included. Maybe we've had trauma where being rejected was the first sign of imminent danger. Maybe it's because it hurts, and we will do just about anything to prevent ourselves from needing to acknowledge that hurt.

Facing our fear of rejection head-on by better understanding how we react to hearing "no" and learning some skills to soothe ourselves when we feel anxious and hurt without lashing out can offer us a more grounded perspective. It's a lot easier to say "thank you for your no" when we can reassure ourselves that the "no" doesn't mean we don't have value.

....

Prompt: Many people struggle to hear "no" because they feel it's a judgment—whether that's a judgment of their request, their morals, or their deserving. Think about a time you heard "no." What did you feel in your body? What thoughts came into your head? How did your heart feel?

Day Twelve:
How Can We Reframe "No"?

One of my favorite sayings is "if you can't say no, your yes doesn't mean anything." I have learned over the years to think of the word "no" as a positive indication of trust. The person telling me that knows I am a safe person to advocate for themselves to. They aren't so afraid of the consequences of saying "no" to me. This also lets me trust their "yes" as honest.

Therefore, I have to admit, I love to say "no." I love to hear "no," too. "No" is like a tidy fence that clearly marks the separation between me and someone else, which feels reassuring, like we're both maintaining our boundaries with love and care. After all, what's the point of a fence if people can walk through it?

But I wasn't always that way. Our society really pushes us to be nice, to say yes to things when we don't really mean it. I used to feel such intense anxiety when a request was made of me that I often said yes as a knee-jerk reaction just to get out of the situation. I would figure out how I felt later.

Zach Budd, Gulf Coast Area advocate for the National Coalition for Sexual Freedom, writes:

> In my consent workshops, I teach that we (by "we" I refer to all people, primarily those of us in Western [colonized] societies) have a strange relationship with the word "no." We have learned that it is

inherently a negative, a dismissal, that it is always impolite. It is charged with judgment. Indeed, it is the case that people have been murdered for saying no to someone who considered rejection an insult. And there are many examples of times when aggressors have taken the capability to say no from their victims.

Thus, we live in a society made up of many people who have been socialized and conditioned to be averse to saying no.

In such a society, one where people have literally been in physical danger for saying no, any time someone is willing to say no to a person, it is an indicator of trust. The person saying no is implying that they trust the person they are saying no to to accept it respectfully. In other words, being told no is a COMPLIMENT! The correct response to being told no is "thank you."

There are lots of reasons we may feel pushed to say yes when we'd rather not. Guilt, fear, and survival are all reasons we might agree to things we don't want to do. This is perhaps part of why there was a campaign at universities to center enthusiastic consent in discussions of sexual consent—it encouraged people to think about what they're excited to do instead of what would make them feel bad if they refused.

Feeling pressured to say yes made me a bad friend for a while. I would become avoidant and flaky when I felt overwhelmed by all the things I agreed to, and my mental health suffered. Even when I did follow through with my commitments, I often wasn't at my best. I began to realize that my feelings of suicidality were less about depression, and more about a desperation to have a goddamned break from people asking things of me.

After that epiphany, I began to practice saying no as a form of self-care. Soon I realized that modeling my own "no" helped those around me feel more comfortable doing so too. Good fences really can make good neighbors.

· ·

Prompt: What are some ways you can communicate to someone, both verbally and with your body language, that "no" is a safe and acceptable answer?

....
....
....
....
....
....
....
....
....
....
....
....
....
....
....
....
....
....
....
....
....
....
....
....
....
....
....
....
....
....
....
....

Day Thirteen:
Can Consent Be Sexy?

When I first started talking about consent culture, many people shortened it to pithy phrases like "consent is sexy." Initially I found it frustrating that people felt the need to make consent sexy in order for them to care about it—after all, consent is mandatory, or should be.

Then I started doing consent classes and I realized how few people had any models for flirtatious or playful consent negotiations. Most of our media pushes this idea that when the moment or behavior is right, you'll "just know." A lot of media also pushes the "she starts out not liking it, but then she warms up to it," which is a dangerous thing to teach people. I definitely went on dates where people recoiled when I asked if it was OK to kiss them or to hold their hand, because they felt that verbalizing my desires took the magic out of them.

That's a misunderstanding waiting to happen, and it doesn't have to be so formalized and awkward.

Avens O'Brien, psychedelic educator and board member of Feminists for Liberty, writes:

> I understand why people get uncomfortable about asking for consent in a moment when things are escalating sexually. First, it can be awkward and can break the mood. Second, there's this social

assumption that the "right person" will just "know" what we want. It's not explicitly stated anywhere, but music, movies, and culture all give us this feeling. It can make us feel like maybe the chemistry is off if we aren't capable of reading a partner's mind. The second one is especially silly because when you're getting to know someone, how can you know their mind already?

There are lots of ways to be playful, spontaneous, and romantic while checking in with a partner to make sure they're comfortable with the escalation.

One of the most romantic nights of my life was a spontaneous night volunteering with a friend I had a very strong crush on. It was a festival in summer, but the night was chilly and we were seated around a campfire, close by and talking.

I mentioned I was chilly and asked if I could sit with him and share our blankets as we talked. He moved to open the blankets to include both the bench beside him and his lap, giving me an option. I said that his lap looked warmest before getting a confirming nod to sit.

We sat there by the fire talking about our lives for literally hours, and I not only felt my own heart beating through my chest, but I swear I could feel his. I looked him in the eyes and asked him, "what would you do if I kissed you right now?" He smiled and said, "I'd kiss you back." I giggled and said, "OK, let's do that," and then I kissed him. It was the most perfect first kiss of my life.

I sometimes think about what I would say to that question if asked by someone I didn't want to kiss. I think it's a romantic move if the answer is affirmative—it doesn't break the mood and it gets both parties excited. In the event that it's a negative, it enables the other party to say no and to offer another option ("I'd give you my cheek," "I'd say I'd like to get to know you better first," "I'd be flattered but I can't," or "I'd be rather surprised because I don't want that.") or to recognize the intention of the asker to escalate and respond accordingly.

Ultimately, I think "what would you do if" is the type of question that doesn't break the mood if the answer is a positive and allows the receiver to set boundaries if the answer is a negative. It also skips the mind-reading but gives you a chance to learn the other person's mind a little bit. We fantasize about a partner who knows what we want without us saying—but we have to teach them first.

I think part of the push toward "it's easier to ask forgiveness than permission" comes back to our unhealthy relationship to accountability. I've seen too many interactions where non-verbal cues were misread and the person who tried to engage physically with another (a kiss, a hug, whatever) responded that they got mixed signals from the other person, so it wasn't *their* fault. I've also heard from friends who were frustrated that a partner didn't do something that the friend didn't communicate, because the partner "should have known."

Clear verbal consent means that each person takes accountability for their own behavior. That's uncomfortable when we want to wriggle out of that accountability by having someone else to blame.

I began to teach folks how I negotiate sexy play with someone, offering "what would you do if" open-ended questions as part of my banter and whispering in someone's

ear, "I would like to _____. What do you think about that?"
It's not perfect—someone could still be uncomfortable and
not answer, or they could answer in a people-pleasing way
instead of one based on their own desires. But it gives an
opening for a negotiation to happen without pulling out a
checklist or having a formal meeting about it.

I still find the focus on sexy, enthusiastic consent poten-
tially problematic because consent doesn't have to be sexy or
enthusiastic for it to still be vital. However, I now understand
that it's important for people to hear that talking about consent also doesn't have to be formulaic, unnatural, or boring.

....

Prompt: I don't believe consent has to be sexy, but it can be!
How do you eroticize conversations about consent? What
makes communication about consent playful or sexy for you?
What methods turn you off? Do you prefer to do it in advance
or as you go? How do you renegotiate during? What are some
ways that your methods could be misconstrued? What are
some ways you could confirm that you're on the same page
without breaking the mood?

Day Fourteen:
Do You Need a Soap Box, a
Tissue Box, or a Tool Box?

We shouldn't just use these ideas about consent with physical touch, but also with emotional consent. When someone is telling me about something that is giving them distress, I've learned not to volunteer advice, but to ask if they would like advice, sympathy, or just to be heard. This puts the power in the hands of the person struggling, giving them autonomy even as they're having a hard time and may not feel empowered.

A little story of how this looks in practice:

> I have learned to start every single Facebook post with a request for advice, sympathy, or just to be heard. Too many times I've posted a rant about a situation that I've already thought about, rolled around in my mind figuring out all the angles and possibilities, only to have a bunch of people give me their (often unexpert) advice. This happens a lot when it comes to things like relationship issues or health troubles, where the general audience doesn't necessarily have context but wants to offer advice anyway. It's a situation that's frustrating for me as the person going through something, but it's

also frustrating for my friends, who want to help and don't understand why I'm annoyed!

By putting my request up front, I create a space where my boundary is clearly communicated, helping my friends help me in a way that I am prepared and ready to receive. It cuts down on my stress and their labor, so we all feel good about the support given.

I tend to believe that people want to help in the best way they know how. Fair enough—offering unsolicited advice is so common it's become a social norm, even if that's not always (or even usually) the best policy. We want to fix the other person's life so they're not in pain, which is a sweet thing to want to do.

However, I suspect that people often want to give advice rather than just listen, and that this is not for my sake, but for theirs. They want to feel useful without asking themselves if they are, in fact, being useful. People get defensive and upset when you say "I just want to feel heard, I don't want to have to discuss in depth the solutions or the issues with those solutions," which underlines my belief that the giving of advice is often not for the person in pain, but for the person who wants to give the advice.

The Art of Seduction by Robert Greene is a book about how to manipulate people. It classifies rescuers as victim types. People who want to help and who base helping as part of their identity will often ensure they are surrounded by people they perceive as in need of help, whether or not those people actually are. The desire to help can be genuinely kind, but it can also quickly turn into a burnout-causing form of codependency.

Additionally, many people are dealing with frustrating situations that don't have a solution because they're institutional problems (for example, not being able to access mental health care because you can't afford it, and the reason you can't afford it is because you are struggling with your mental health and that makes getting a decently paying job harder). To an outsider, it may look like someone complaining over and over again about a situation that seems like it can be fixed by a lifestyle change, or a change of attitude, or better communication. For the person in the struggle, hearing the same advice from a dozen different people can invalidate their lived experience. I'm thinking here of how many times people told me my back issues could be solved through eating more kale and doing yoga, when in fact I had a birth defect in my spine that needed medical intervention. They meant well, but I had tried those things to no avail, and really just needed space to rant.

If you're truly going to be present for someone, you have to be willing to meet people where they're at, and also take care of yourself and your boundaries.

....

Prompt: Can you think of a time where you would have preferred sympathy instead of advice, or to be heard instead of sympathy? How did you feel when you got support, but not the support you hoped for? Did you tell the other person?

WEEK THREE: OUR RELATIONSHIP TO THE COMMUNITY

We've explored consent and our relationship to it within ourselves, and we've touched on consent in dynamics between us and another person. But consent also has to do with our wider communities. It can be especially contentious and complicated in spaces where subtle (or even blatant) coercion is often built into the system, like in the workplace, in medical settings, in schools, or in the prison/industrial complex of our legal system. Places where an uneven power dynamic is part of the structure often include situations where our full, freely given, informed consent is pushed to the side, and if we want or need to engage in that structure to, say, make rent or have access to medication, we have to go along with it.

It's also something that comes up a lot in activism. I've been doing mutual aid work like helping in houseless encampments, acting as a street medic, and doing direct action protests for most of my adult life. I have learned that consent is a complex beast when it comes to what actions the group chooses to do, and how it shakes out on the ground. As a street medic, I have been at protests that turned violent, and while I was not giving enthusiastic consent to be in that situation, I felt obliged to carry through my duty to care for the wounded. I've also witnessed issues in spaces like Occupy where white cisgender men often assigned themselves positions of leadership where they could control accountability processes and often considered themselves above the agreements of the group. Obviously, that wasn't particularly safe or sustainable.

There's an agreement I truly hate in *The Four Agreements* by Don Miguel Ruiz. It's a spiritual guidance self-help book with four main statements: Be Impeccable With Your Word, Don't Take Anything Personally, Don't Make Assumptions, and Always Do Your Best. On the surface, these all seem pretty sensible. But I have an issue with the second one.

The "wisdom" clarifying the statement is that nothing other people do is because of you. Rather, it's because of their own lives and experiences, so you shouldn't take it personally. I see the appeal there. It's very individualistic and gives us a lot of control—after all, we're all only responsible for ourselves and our behavior.

I think this is true to some extent. But I've also seen this reasoning used all too often to blame victims for responding to their abuse in the ways that make them feel safe—like having a boundary wouldn't be necessary if you could just let other people's behavior roll off your back. I think that this approach minimizes the power dynamics in place in a white supremacist capitalist patriarchy, which only serves to further the inequity between those with the most power and those with the least. And, perhaps worst of all, this approach feels like it seeks to assign blame, making accountability feel like a weight to be avoided instead of a gift to help you learn and grow.

This week is all about applying what you've learned and your critical thinking consent skills to interactions with your community at large, whether you're a church volunteer, an anarchist soup kitchen organizer, a sex party host, a book club host, or all of the above. We'll think about how to create a safe and transparent container, how to hold people accountable with compassion but also with follow-through, and how we define community in the first place.

Day Fifteen:
Who Is Your Community?

The word "community" gets presented a lot when discussing a group of people who share an identity or interest of some type: the LGBTQ+ community, the gaming community, the kink community, etc. It's assumed that these groups, however large and amorphous they may be, are part of a united front in some capacity. A feeling of fellowship in sharing something in common is a wonderful thing.

Usually, however, these groups struggle when it comes to accountability. I believe this is in part because while they share *something* (whether that be a fandom, a neighborhood, or an identity), they don't necessarily share morals, ideals, or goals. I, for example, am part of the wider LGBTQ+ community. This community may also include, say, a gay man who is a right-wing provocateur. Outside of being LGBTQ+, we may have no shared values or touchstones. Therefore, I would not consider us in community with one another. How could I hold this person accountable (or vice versa) if we don't have respect for each other or care about upsetting one another? I think it's important for community to be intentional and curated, not just a bunch of people with a common identity or interest.

Angelique Luna, kink-aware and conscious erotic touch professional, writes:

Many social groups are just to get together to be part of a conversation or activity—without any vetting, deep commitment, or policing of one another. There's no investment in each other. Therefore, it can be easy in a group setting to feel lost or judged by another member without any accountability, and a bad experience can alienate you entirely.

Most communities, however, have some element of policing, and while there usually isn't a specific person charged with this task, it usually occurs naturally. For example, if a member exhibits behavior that does harm to a community, they may be warned or ignored as a result. Essentially, rejected by the other members. This may be for illegal activity or language or behavior that goes against the spirit of the community.

A few years ago, my husband and I created a bisexual men's support group for men and their supporters (spouses, partners, friends, etc.). The mission was to have a safe space to talk about their experiences, talk about the challenges they were having, and other miscellaneous issues or situations they were dealing with.

It was a challenge to have men attend the meetings due to fear of being out to society. Our Meetup.com group had over six hundred members, but barely ten men would attend the in-person meetings. We did our very best to keep trolls out of the group or anyone just looking for a hookup, as there were enough apps and websites for this. For those who did attend the meetings, they did create their little community. We supported each other by listening, giving advice, and sharing our own experiences. We may have started a group but did become a community.

I belong to many groups for my career as well as socially, and they have proven very useful and beneficial. However, the communities I claim to belong to have my vested interest and commitment. I try my best to support the members of my communities and have sometimes relied on them for support.

I also find the word "community" is thrown around a lot as a substitute for other relationships, particularly in the world of media and marketing. Facebook "communities" can be anything from a brand fan group to social media followers to people who come to a monthly event. They can be a starting place for a richer type of community, but they aren't inherently communities—genuine communities, in my opinion, require tending.

I prefer to make my own definition of community small and intimate. To me, a community has mutual care, mutual accountability, and mutual responsibility. It's something we opt into. We call each other in or out as needed because we feel invested in improving each other as people. We care about each other, not in a vague "I care about all humans" kind of way but in an active solidarity kind of way. We put in work, and we trust each other. There's a real relationship there.

But my definition is just my own. I encourage you to reflect on the communities you're in, and what support you get from them. What makes them communities for you?

....

Prompt: How do you define community for yourself? How would you differentiate a community from a group of people with a shared identity or interest?

Day Sixteen:
Who Can You Process
Boundary Crossing With?

Trust is a scary thing. Pretty much every person I've talked to about it has experienced putting their trust into a loved one, a friend, a coworker, a boss, or even an institution, only to find that trust completely shattered into bits. It can be disappointing at the mildest level, and deeply traumatic at the most intense. Trust requires some vulnerability and honesty, and when that's been violated it can be difficult to rebuild.

Trust also takes time. I remember once as a teen feeling unheard and unseen, and, in a pique, stealing some money from one of my parents' wallets. I got caught, and I had to write some sentences as an apology, and that was that. But after having broken my parents' trust, I was really annoyed that despite being disciplined, I didn't automatically get that trust back. I had apologized, after all—why wasn't that enough??

Well, I had to work for it and demonstrate integrity. Each time I broke trust, it took longer to rebuild. I had to show that I said what I meant, and meant what I said, through my respectful behaviors. I didn't get to decide when that trust was earned—as the people I had hurt, my parents set the pace.

That said, we did the work to trust and be vulnerable with each other over the years. Now, my parents are some of the first people I talk to when processing a situation. I trust their judgment, but I also trust them to hold me accountable while also having my back. They'll tell me if I'm the asshole, but they'll also still love me and support me in working on myself. I'm not afraid to be wrong in front of them, and our values are similar enough that I feel safe aligning my integrity with theirs.

Such trust and vulnerability were important aspects to the relationship I sought out when I picked my sobriety sponsor. I wanted someone who shared my values so that they would kindly but firmly call me on my shit. I feel safe making mistakes and being corrected by her, so I can be my honest, truest self. And I know if I needed her support, I would have it—not because she does what I want, but because she cares about me and trusts me.

If I'm really honest, there aren't many people I have that level of trust and intimacy with.

Yael R. Rosenstock Gonzalez, Puerto Rican Jewish pleasure activist and owner of SexPositiveYou, writes:

> As a young teen, I was in a sexually coercive and emotionally abusive relationship that left me with a plethora of emotional and sexual triggers. I've been in multiple relationships since, where the gut reaction to my being triggered tended to be more defensiveness than understanding.
>
> One night, my now husband crossed a boundary that he had misunderstood, and I broke down in tears. I was afraid he would dismiss me or be angry because partners before had responded that way. Instead, he told me my feelings were valid and asked if I wanted to talk about it or just cry. He assured me that I didn't owe him an explanation—it was enough to know that I was not OK and that we would work

to make sure this trigger was avoided in the future, whether I chose to share the story behind it or not.

The safety and care exuded by his response calmed my anxious mind and let me know it's OK for me to not be OK. Though for years I had been silent and let myself be retraumatized, by this point I was used to telling people when my boundaries were being crossed but would do so with great discomfort because I'd be consumed with concern about how that person might feel about my expressing a boundary. This moment showed me that if the person is centering my well-being rather than their feelings about my feelings (which is how it should be), then I don't need to fear retribution, resentment, nor defensiveness.

This lesson hasn't quite calmed my nerves for when I express my boundaries to others, but it has left me hopeful that more people will respond similarly (and some do!). Because I know my feelings are heard and validated, and that we will work together to find solutions as issues arise, I feel safe, and that has been incredibly healing.

Over the years, I realized that when I looked closely, a lot of "communities" I was a part of didn't have a sense of fellowship, and that I also often actively didn't trust the people stewarding them. It made me rethink my relationships with those groups and helped me center keeping myself in check when I was a leader in communities of my own. One method I ended up using was having a diverse board in charge of events instead of one or two people, in the hopes that someone who was seeking accountability from a member of the board would be more likely to click with one board member. I'm also a huge fan of anonymous feedback, which can feel safer than open feedback. These methods aren't perfect, but I hope that they will make it feel more comfortable for my community members to address issues, including issues with me.

....

Prompt: Who do you feel safe with when processing situations where your boundaries were crossed? What helps you feel safe talking to this person? Is there someone in a leadership position in your communities who provides a similar feeling of safety?

....
....
....
....
....
....
....
....
....
....
....
....
....
....
....
....
....
....

....
....
....
....
....
....
....
....
....
....
....
....
....
....
....
....
....
....
....
....
....
....
....
....
....
....
....
....
....
....

Day Seventeen:
What Do You Do When
Society Is Coercive?

When I was doing some research on this question, I was pretty horrified to see articles that said things like "Is it OK to say no at work? Sometimes" and "Your childbirth rights —how to say no, nicely." I recoiled at the idea that you should have to be delicate about your boundaries around your time or your body to avoid offending others.

Unfortunately though, we live in a society where we are pressured to say yes as often as possible with a big smile on our faces, no matter how little we want to. And workplaces are not communities in the way that I define them (there isn't mutual care, mutual accountability, and mutual responsibility, at least in most workplaces). Yet we are encouraged to feel beholden to them as if they are.

One of my friends anonymously writes:

> I was on a date.
>
> He was a person who worked on the COVID-19 research and casefile data, during pre-vaccine COVID-19. A premier contributor at a prestigious and internationally collaborative university, as they all were then, collaborating for the cure. He was a PhD mired in regressions that contributed greatly to the pattern unraveling required to develop a vaccine.

In form and in spirit he was the type of man I would seduce after three glasses of wine. Except, with the space COVID created, I had the time to discern I actually wasn't that into him. Yes, we had wine. Yes, three glasses. Yes, I absolutely wanted the science, camaraderie, and laughter we were sharing. It was fun and six-feet-distanced. We were laughing a lot about the new emerging Zoom culture. We talked about how to shoot a perfect free throw. He talked (and perhaps hovered too long) about how his basketball team partied in high school.

He made for a great potential dinner-party guest, but in the space created by COVID, I had time to discern that whatever light of his Indiana high school basketball days should have glowed from within was not aglow for me.

After three hours of uplifting discourse, he asked me for a kiss as I walked him from the balcony, past the kitchen, and amiably to the door. I said no to the kiss. I shrugged, shook my head, and said, "Nah. Not tonight."

And he said, "Oh, you don't want to kiss because of COVID?" I replied, "Oh, yes. You got it. I don't want to kiss because of COVID."

He said, "I totally understand" and amiably left. Not even expecting or attempting a weird conciliatory hug. That is when I realized how much COVID Has My Back™. Dating during this pandemic, I wouldn't have to do anything—no touching—and that would be expected. That is when I realized that the Victorian Era dating ethos of being hands-off, intentional, and six feet apart (which had emerged as the acceptable dating culture during these unprecedented times) absolutely served me. The six-foot distance and a dominant paradigm of consent before any touching was a gift for me.

The interaction made me realize that even though I think I am great at "conflict" and saying "no" and "being the right size" or "taking up space," the relief that swept over my body when he assumed my no wasn't about him was a huge reveal. I was so relieved he thought I was rejecting him because of the pandemic circumstances.

If not for COVID, I probably would have kissed him out of some self-inflicted or culturally coercive norm that "if you have a good time, you kiss." I absolutely would have unconsciously genuflected to some requirement of preserving his experience rather than saying no. This interaction proved an inspiration for me. How can I live, always, with the assumption that COVID Has My Back™? Or, perhaps better stated, how can I live my life as if someone will not take my rejection personally and that they'll actually celebrate my saying no?

The ethereal license his response gave me was inebriating. And funny, in a way, since COVID was the last reason I didn't smooch him. I just wasn't into him like that. It let me know that despite "the work" I did when learning about consent culture, there were a lot of my own unconscious leanings actively acting against my most authentic emotion of "nope."

Consent culture taught me that when a marine kissed me on the dance floor in 1998, he should have asked. I was taken aback by his mouth on me, but as they say, I went with it. It taught me that my emotionally "tough" posture, as a five-foot-eleven female athlete, could not protect me. Lifting weights and having a healthy body image made me no less a target when I was overpowered by a professional basketball player and raped in 2001. It allowed me to adjust my thesis that being born into a body that was larger than most women did not require that I lose sight of the fact that I too am susceptible to being treated like a woman, to being harmed like one.

Consent culture helped me to be soft and admit that I do not know how to properly guard myself against my own maladaptive fawning responses in an inherently violent society.

COVID also gave me a powerful awareness tool: relief. I was relieved that the pandemic created 1. an assumption of personal space while I was on dates, 2. culturally accepted guidance as to how much space, and 3. the concept of asking permission before touching. In the relief I felt, I became aware I am usually bracing against a dating culture and likely suitors that assume my "no" is a problem. The temporary norm of distance, awareness, and consent before physical touch was a relief, I determined, because it was so unfamiliar.

In my COVID circles, "no" was invited. "No thank you" was assumed. And "celebrating no" was a phenomenon of COVID that I continue to share with potential partners.

Currently, I'm experimenting with "dating lessons from a Victorian-era pandemic" as part of a standup bit I'm writing. I contemplate the celebration of "no" as the dominant paradigm rather than the coercion to "yes." I contemplate how to preserve these tenets of space in my body and my voice, even without a mask, or the trappings of global pandemic collapse to protect me.

It is easier to get some sort of justice and accountability within my community, but I also still live in a wider society that regularly reminds me it doesn't owe me shit. There is a demand that people who are being taken advantage of or abused "remain civil," as if that would stop the bad behavior. Yet all too often, taking the high road means ignoring people who are verbally abusing you in the hopes that they'll leave you alone if you don't engage. If you stand up for yourself, you are told that you shouldn't validate bullies with a response and scolded for how you chose to take action, like it's your fault you're being bullied in the first place. "Don't make a scene," "it's just a joke," and "they didn't mean it" all put the focus on how the victim behaves instead of how the abuser behaves, and that coerces victims into silence and shame.

I have been threatened on social media, had my address publicized and my loved ones harassed, my coworkers pressured to get me fired, and the SWAT team called on me, so I personally disagree that civility is the answer in all cases. In my experience, "ignoring it" can cause bullies to escalate until they get your attention. I suspect that the calls for civility and turning the other cheek often come from people who are scared to stand up against bullying themselves when they witness it, and they don't want to feel guilty or complicit. This creates a catch-22 system of coercion, wherein you are damned if you say stop, and damned if you let it continue.

Being aware of this has caused me to reframe how I ask people for things I need. I often ask if something would be possible, making it a question open to counteroffers. I also always reassure the person that no is an acceptable response, and that I can make things work without the favor, so they have an out if they want it. When someone at work asks me to do something I can't do (or even just don't want to do), I now say "I'm afraid I can't do that, but here's what I can do," whether they left room to negotiate or not. My polite but firm resistance to coercion makes it clear that my boundaries are to be respected, and I feel more empowered.

That said, I am also a freelancer and a white woman with a middle-class upbringing, even if I have a working-class adulthood. I have a lot of freedom to make a counteroffer, or to walk away from a situation that doesn't serve me. When I was doing sex work, I was my own boss, so I could choose my clients and I could leave if I felt uncomfortable. The more marginalized you are, the harder it is to protect your boundaries without negative consequences impacting you.

That, to me, is also part of the system of coercion that makes it OK for some people to say no but not others.

....

Prompt: What are some ways our society creates a system of coercion? When have you wanted to say no to a social ask (at work, in a social setting, at the hospital) but didn't? Did you feel safe saying no? What made you feel safe or unsafe?

Day Eighteen:
When Can Consent Be Complex?

One of the things I encounter a lot when talking to people about consent and writing about consent is a real craving for One Right Answer in every situation. Preferably, people want One Right Answer that can be reliably applied to multiple situations. Unfortunately, that would rely on multiple things that aren't true: that there is always an objective truth, that everyone is on an equal playing field, and that interpretations of behavior (including our own interpretations of our own behavior) are accurate.

A personal anecdote to illustrate what I mean:

> I personally find it really complex to wrestle with situations in which an individual may consent to a risky decision but the consequence of that decision impacts others who may not be consenting. One example is smoking. While I may have consented to the risks and harms of smoking a cigarette, I tried to ensure that other people weren't in the way of my smoke. I asked people before smoking and where it was OK to do so, and I picked up my butts so I didn't leave a mess. My consent did not and should not have overridden the consent of those around me, especially since it had the potential to impact them indirectly.

I'm writing this in 2022, after two years of the deadly, worldwide, airborne pandemic COVID-19. I have wrestled a lot with my feelings about mask mandates as an infectious disease nerd, as an anarchist who distrusts the government's intentions, as an anti-racist who is well aware of the history of medical malpractice toward Black and brown folks, and as a consent educator.

As I write, we are in the middle of yet another wave of this pandemic, and yet masks to prevent the spread have become optional. Businesses can set their own standards for both their customers and their workers. People with disabilities are told to just stay home, as if that's a long-term option, as if it's our fault if we get sick, as if anyone even fully understands the lasting effects of long COVID.

I find myself heavily conflicted, holding two seemingly disparate opinions—I believe that people should have bodily autonomy, and I also believe that infectious disease does not care about or respect boundaries.

There are so many places where people share space—school, work, stores, public transit—that it's unavoidable to be in communal spaces with people who refuse to get vaccinated or wear a mask. Each person who willingly doesn't get vaccinated or refuses to wear a mask raises the risk level for everyone else (especially people who can't get vaccinated for medical reasons), and this is nonconsensual risk. Workers have been assaulted for asking customers to wear masks as per store policy, and many employees don't get a say on whether they're allowed to mask up at work themselves. Whose consent matters in these situations?

With all this in mind, do I think that governments should force vaccines? No, that also makes me uncomfortable from a consent perspective. I guess where I've landed is that I wish people had information that allowed them to make scientifically accurate, informed decisions, that kept them and those around them safe. But until common sense is common, I'm still wrestling with how much enforcement is and should be OK.

There are a lot of things that can impact and influence consent. Capability to consent is one such thing. Substance use is often pointed to as an example of this, and it's a significant one, but being in an emotional state, such as while grieving and vulnerable, can also impact your ability to clearly consent. Lack of sleep, low blood sugar, mental health issues or physical disability can also get in the way of a clear yes or no. Financial independence, marginalization and power dynamics, feeling like you have time to think of your answer, whether or not the context is informed and honest—all of these layers create complex consent dynamics.

There are also situations where my consent and someone else's consent are diametrically opposed. The above mask situation is a good real-life example of this, where both people's autonomy cannot be fully respected at the same time. In situations like this, I often make my assessment of who to prioritize according to what has the potential for more indirect harm, who has more ability to opt out of the situation, and who has more power in the interaction. It's not a perfect metric, but it often gives me the information I need to make a reasonable conclusion.

Don't get me wrong, I often wish I had One Right Answer. I'd sleep a lot better! But I just don't think it's ethically or philosophically possible. What do you think?

....

Prompt: Can you think of any examples of situations with complex, layered consent? Have you been in a situation where your consent and someone else's consent were opposite responses? What's something you can do to advocate for consent in that situation (both yours and other people's)?

Day Nineteen:
How Do Communities Respond?

It's very human to look at how one community deals with consent violations and boundary crossing and be able to identify how it was done wrong. It's also very human to not be entirely sure how to do it right, or what "right" even means. Right for whom?

Nazelah Jamison, performance poet, actress, and vocalist, writes:

> The poetry communities that I have been a part of tend to be pretty indignantly righteous. Long before the #MeToo movement was in the forefront, the national poetry slam community had our own sort of "public calling out" of people in our community who had been inappropriate or violated consent.
>
> Initially, it was helpful. The first few people named had pretty questionable if not downright dangerous behaviors, and the so-called calling outs made us all aware of this so that we could protect ourselves. Like all things, though, and especially with a community of individuals as vocal and attention-seeking as poets tend to be, it soon grew into a competition of who could be the most publicly righteous.

People started being called out for mundane "offenses," like staring at someone too long, or being a bit too persistent asking for a date. Actions that, while they may induce discomfort or be a little intimidating, didn't rise to the level of assault or even necessarily harassment. And yet, anything called out was immediately assumed to be and thus escalated to rape, and the demand was that the accused be shunned, alienated, and forgotten. Anyone who remained their friend or ally was accused of being a rape apologist.

Unlike incarceration, where a person does their time and is released, there was no end date to this punishment. Even if the accused made all of the amends and demonstrated growth, repentance, and personal change, they were indefinitely labeled a rapist. A few people I love permanently lost community and livelihood over situations that did not rise to the level of sexual assault or harassment. When a few victims recanted, it was kept very quiet. Names were destroyed, but not redeemed, in public.

I don't know what the solution is, but it is definitely not what we did. I believe that, yes, a community should be warned when there are dangerous people in their midst. Sure, if someone endangers a community member, then that person should be prevented from causing more harm in that community. But not every situation is cut and dry, and binary solutions for every incident are counterproductive. Sometimes, it is very clear what happened and someone is 100% in the wrong, but most situations aren't like this. Sometimes, both parties are intoxicated and neither remembers who initiated or what happened. Sometimes, the accused party walked away completely unaware of their own wrongdoing, because they missed or ignored the "no," or it wasn't clearly given.

There are people in this world who have truly bad intentions. But I think most people are simply humans who make (sometimes heinous) mistakes and missteps. I think we've figured out that we can't make humans disappear just because we disapprove of their actions. When we try, inevitably people reoffend elsewhere, or harm themselves, or go away temporarily but come back the same or worse. I believe that we should never stop discussing solutions and working toward creating processes and solutions as individual as the situations that we are seeking to solve.

When I started doing workshops about consent culture, I found myself at the forefront of these discussions a lot. Everyone agreed that when harm was done, the person harmed deserved care and the person who did the harm needed to be held accountable. But what did that *mean?* Communities often tore themselves apart arguing over what the formula should be in every situation, trying to narrow down what exactly "care" looked like, what "centering the victim" meant in practical terms, and even more so, what "accountability" meant.

I saw an uncomfortable truth in how this manifested. "Accountability" in practical terms often meant something different for heterosexual white men than it did for trans women, or Black men, or any number of folks who were more marginalized.

Heterosexual white men often got an accountability pod, usually of white women who empathized with him and felt he was "doing his best." Often, the idea was that the heterosexual white man who had done wrong would be held to understand what he had done, educate himself on how to do better, and then demonstrate more trustworthy behaviors. But again, what does any of that actually mean? There's no certificate to show that you've done the work. As for the people doing the job of holding him accountable? Well, being a part of an accountability pod looks like a stressful unpaid second job, something that was often left to femmes to do, which is another layer of issue with this approach. Eventually the pod would stop writing updates for the community and the process would either see the pod become apologists for the guy's fuckups, or it would just fizzle out because no one could be bothered.

For marginalized people, though, the answer was almost always ostracization and banishment. If you wanted to get someone labeled dangerous and kicked out of a community, all you had to do is say they were abusive and that person would be blacklisted. I watched trans women, especially, get bullied out of jobs and homes for incredibly vague accusations against them in the name of accountability, often by people more privileged than them. To question this was seen as not supporting the victim. To me, this process was encouraging a cycle where the abused sometimes became the abuser. I don't see that as especially helpful.

So now, when I think about a community accountability process, I think about some concrete steps that the person can take to show good faith attempts to improve and evolve. I think about a timeline for stepping back from positions of power so the person can focus on their internal work—a timeline that has an end point where, dependent on their growth, they can begin to mend what they broke in a community that knows exactly what red flags to keep an eye out for. I think about what the behaviors were, defining them, getting as specific as possible so it's clear if the line has been crossed. And I ask the person harmed what would help them feel safe, offering some potential solutions as options to decrease their feeling overwhelmed. Sometimes, a person needs to be fully kicked out and other communities need to be warned against them. But that's a last resort, not the first choice. It's not a perfect system, but it allows for some flexibility within a structure, and it's been useful in communities I manage currently.

....

Prompt: How do your communities handle situations where boundaries are crossed? Are they transparent about how they come to a solution? Do you feel this process works? Do you feel it could be improved?

Day Twenty:
How Can We Create a
Code of Conduct?

This prompt is all about the rubber hitting the road. While a lot of my personal experience with this is around community leadership and organizing, communicating expectations concisely and clearly is something to consider whether it's around a long-standing social justice network or a dinner party. It's easy to say to yourself that you want people to show up more, but what does that look like in a practical sense? And how do you communicate those expectations or intentions in a way that speaks the language of the people in the group, adding to the culture in a harmonious way rather than in a jarring change of tone?

I experienced this myself when I decided to throw a birthday party at my house:

> When I threw my first party at my house, I didn't think to make any rules—it was just a birthday party. Who makes guidelines for a birthday party?
>
> Except, then a couple ended up having sex in one of the two bathrooms for a half hour, and the other bathroom was being too often used as a place to do drugs. I'm not against sex or drugs—I'm pretty pro both really—but I *am* against those activities commandeering the two bathrooms available!

The next time I threw a party at my house, I antic-
ipated this issue and wrote up a code of conduct,
which seemed like a very orderly Capricorn thing to
do (Caps are known for a businesslike demeanor),
but also seemed like a way to get ahead of the issue.
I set aside two spaces, one called Heaven, which was
for quiet hanging out and platonic cuddling, and
one called Hell, which was for more adult stuff.

I let participants know that I was disabling the
bathroom door locks, so if they wanted a private space
at this party, Heaven and Hell were their options.
Obviously, I wanted people to knock on a closed door
before entering, but I also wanted to prevent those
spaces from being closed off to the whole party. I also
had a sign on the bathrooms that cheerily reminded
people to be expedient and respect the space. And it
worked! People used the bathrooms as bathrooms
and the quiet/play spaces as intended, and I didn't
have anyone doing an awkward potty dance.

I think it helped that my tone was an anticipatory
and amused "c'mon, y'all, let's work together here"
versus needing to solve an immediate problem with
higher stakes. And it made me realize that rules can
be fun if you make them something collaborative
instead of something authoritarian. That experience
informed how I made codes of conduct for larger
events later on!

I've hosted full-on sex parties, and I've hosted tabletop
role-playing game nights. There are some similar guidelines
between the two, though they use different terms. For example, a word that communicates a hard stop is what we call
a safe word at a sex party, while in a role-playing game, we

might call it an X card. Of course, there are differences too. While a sex party generally has a code of conduct that was written by the host and people negotiate from there with their partner(s), a tabletop game often has a system called lines and veils, where you all discuss together what you absolutely don't want to have discussed during the game (lines) and what you don't mind being discussed as long as it isn't too detailed and most of the interaction happens "off screen" (veils).

The tone is also important. I probably wouldn't communicate the same exact guidelines in the same way at, say, a rowdy circus-themed party as I would at a peaceful meditation retreat. Even if the gist was the same, tweaking the words to fit the tone—whether playful, thoughtful, mystical, or snarky—will encourage the community to feel more invested and involved.

How you communicate the guidelines is another part of the process. I've been to interactive events where the rules are a call-and-response moment between the stage and the audience. Being able to recite them makes you feel excited for what's to come and feel included in the community. I've been to other fancy-dress events where the rules are presented as a list of manners by a haughty servant as they take your coat. How you actively communicate the rules can be a part of the fun if you invest the time to make it so.

....

Prompt: Even if you aren't in leadership, you can still think about what might and might not be effective in your communities. Brainstorm what an ideal consent culture–focused code of conduct might look like for one of your communities, including ways to call in members of the community and some ways restorative justice could be achieved. What guidelines have you liked in other group codes of conduct? What are five guidelines you might include for your community?

Day Twenty-One:
How Can We Improve
Community Care?

When I first came into the kink community, I felt it took itself Very Seriously in a way that not only made me feel predated on as a young submissive, but also straight-up bored. I wanted to go to events that allowed for heavier play (and less alcohol) than a nightclub, but I also wanted to wear silly outfits and play music that wasn't either Enya or industrial. It was only about a year after I moved to California before I was organizing my own events as a twenty-year-old, trying to figure out how to make the power imbalance of being an organizer transparent while also challenging the idea of a hierarchy.

It was through my experiments that I had the basis for writing my first ideas on what community leaders could do to cultivate consent culture in their communities, publishing my thoughts via the Consent Culture Project. At that point (2011), I had a few years under my belt running a large sex party, Kinky Salon London, and had been implementing my theories about consent culture dynamics at those events. I included tips like "don't just have your rules written down, interact with people as they walk in the door to make going over the rules part of the lead-up to a fun night," and "make sure your hosts are accessible and diverse, so even a shy newbie can feel safe talking to them." They seemed like obvious points to me, but for many they were revolutionary.

Zach Budd, Gulf Coast Area advocate for the National Coalition for Sexual Freedom, writes:

> In some of the online communities (poly, kink, swinger) that I am in, a standing rule is to always ask before proceeding with an action that may affect another. So, if someone shares a picture, one asks before commenting. Group members must get consent before directly messaging someone.
>
> I have introduced the practice of asking before saving a picture someone sends to me via phone or social media. I do this because the sending of photos ought not to imply the consent to save said photo in one's device. That is something that I'm always surprised to hear that people have never heard before. If someone sends me a photo of anything, I will ask if they want me to dispose of the photo or ask permission to save it. Most people I've encountered have never been presented with this option. I firmly believe that a consent culture should be one in which fewer things are implied.

When you first start bringing consent-focused suggestions to a community, there might be some pushback. You'd be amazed how resistant people were when I initially proposed event organizers train their volunteers as first responders for sexual assault disclosure or having a town hall for organizers to meet up regularly to talk about policies that were and weren't working in their spaces.

I began to understand why that resistance was happening as I began to notice who was funding and running various events. Oftentimes someone who was dominant, male, white, cis, and "popular" (or some combination of most of the above) was the person who was "in charge" of the event or the space, or often both. The people who owned the venues were typically people who had come up in whisper campaigns as creepy or even abusive, and they were often friends with the event organizers, many of whom had their own complaints lodged against them. Even ethical people who genuinely wanted these events to be safer and more transparent felt trapped by their need for the only affordable venues and/or the blessing of the larger-event organizers.

Now, I learned that I couldn't control how other people ran their events or where they called home. What I could do, however, was model what I wanted to see in my community. And while my events weren't perfect, I did try very hard to be open to feedback, including (especially) when the feedback was harsh and hard to hear. Several people who called me out for my ignorance or my sloppiness ended up becoming friends who trusted me to take their comments on board and improve in the future. That behind-the-scenes accountability was as important to me as the event itself, and it created a standard that other events began to strive toward.

It's also important to remember that as a community member, you also have some power. You can listen to those who are harmed and lend your shoulder and voice to them if they desire it. You can stick to your negotiations, rather than trying to push a little further and get a little more out of a partner or a volunteer. You can call out bullshit when you see it, loudly and clearly, which will not only offer solidarity to the person harmed, but also encourage others around you to speak up. We are all potential leaders when it comes to modeling ethical behavior, whether or not we serve the community directly in that way at that moment.

Prompt: What's one way the communities you are a part of promote and encourage a consent culture? What's something they could improve? What are some strategies that could help them to do so? Is there something in society or in a community that seems like a clear violation of consent but isn't acknowledged or addressed? How could it be addressed?

WEEK FOUR: REFLECTION

We're nearing the finish line of our work together. Congratulations for coming this far! This is hard work and you're doing a great job.

We've talked about understanding ourselves and our relationship to consent, how we negotiate and navigate consent with people close to us, and how we traverse it in our wider communities. My hope is that the questions we've addressed so far will help you create some practical solutions that fit with your culture and your community voice in a way that will encourage a wider adoption of your ideas. Keep in mind that this is a learning and charting process, and you may find that if you revisit some of those questions in a few years, you could have really different answers! This workbook is not to prescribe one true way, but rather to support you in developing or honing critical thinking skills that you can apply to your own, ever-evolving situations.

Now, let's bring this back to ourselves and what we've learned in this process. This workbook is like the ouroboros, a serpent eating its own tail in a symbol of unity and infinity, continuing around and around.

Week one was about introspection and meditation, and this final week is about taking that grounded information and acting upon it from a position of understanding and strength. We'll talk about how to take small steps moving forward. We'll talk about how to make this information accessible across generational boundaries. We'll learn how to be accountable as individuals, building a consent culture, while also being gentle with ourselves and others as people who are learning. I also want you to reflect on how to balance this heavy work and self-care. Consider what that looks like for you and how to manage your priorities to give yourself that push forward but also space to breathe.

Day Twenty-Two:
How Are You Doing?

I often think about the kind of introspection we've been doing in this workbook as exercise for a muscle. Our cultural misunderstanding of consent as a concept is like a tense glute—while you can live with it, it can make going through the world increasingly more difficult and uncomfortable. What I'm hoping to offer here is some gentle stretching, some regular exercise, and some rest and Icy Hot so you can make your consent muscle stronger and more stable, thus improving the rest of your life in a variety of ways.

But just like with exercise, it can be easy to overdo it because we want those end results as quickly as possible. Going too hard, too fast can lead to injury, pain, and a reluctance to engage in that exercise again. Self-care is vital to make sure that you are balancing out the important work with relaxation and compassion. What that looks like is personal to you. Perhaps you only do one prompt a week, or maybe you do the prompts with a therapist so you have a safe person to work through them with you. While writing this book, I gave myself a time limit per day, and when that time limit was over, I cooked myself something nice, which also meant self-care by feeding myself and moving my body around.

Taking care of yourself helps you keep doing the introspection that propels you and your understanding forward! It's rehydration for your brain.

Pete Bailey, mental health occupational therapist, writes:

Until I got my job working in an inpatient psychiatric unit, I could not understand the importance of self-care. I've heard it said that self-care is survival. Every week I go to work and meet someone who just tried to kill themselves and is surprised that they survived the attempt. Every day, a person is contemplating a suicide attempt, experiencing mania or psychosis, or has been actively starving themselves. It's a lot.

Two years ago, my mother died of ALS. The last year of her life was a rapid decline. It all began with a fall that she couldn't get up from. It was clear things were changing, and quickly. I started traveling home at least once a month. Each time, I would see more of her losses. Back in the Bay Area, I had my regular job and a teaching job that I had committed to before knowing what was to come in the year.

I wanted to support my patients, but I also needed to be there for myself. This required some compartmentalization—focus on work at work. Then at home, try to cope with work stress and family stress. There were easy ways to escape from reality or numb out, like drinking, smoking weed, making dirty videos, and having hot sex. Each of which had its place. But I found I needed a lot more support to get through it.

The starting place was focusing on what I could control. Sleep was super important. In general, I struggle with insomnia. So, I cultivated regular routines and set wake and sleep times, which helped. I also focused on eating. When I'm stressed, I tend to undereat or not eat. I've learned that it leads to more problems and I'm less able to keep moving forward. Three meals and two or three snacks in a day lead to even moods and more energy. When it's hard to eat, I buy a lot of simple foods like open-and-heat, bake-in-the-oven, or boil-and-add-sauce items. Also, grab-and-go proteins feed the brain.

My body needs to move! If I get trapped in the past or stuck worrying about the future, the only path back to now is through movement. So I walk with upbeat tunes through the rolling hills of my neighborhood, do body-awareness movements like yoga or Pilates, and sometimes I get funky and turn up some music and dance as weirdly as possible.

I am very fortunate to be part of a community of queers. So many of us have known each other for more than a decade. We truly have had some magical fairy-dust days in that time, but truly sad and horrible things have happened too. All it takes to feel the depth of the community is to put the word out that help is needed. My friends offered meals with them or delivered, hikes, phone calls, hugs, rides to airports, and house-sitting. When my mom died, one dear friend flew to join me at the funeral. Another joined me in Portland, where I simmered down for a week after spending two and a half weeks planning and attending her funeral.

All of these things—sleep, food, movement, and friend support—are essential when life cranks up to a ten on the suck scale. Also, doing something creative daily can lighten things up a lot!

Another tough part about all this is that you might be the first person in your group doing this kind of work in an in-depth way. Or maybe you're trying to catch up to a community around you that seems to have been doing this work for a while, and you feel kind of lost or internally pressured to keep up. You may feel really excited to make changes in your life thanks to the things you're discovering about yourself, and you want that same kind of progress for those around you. It's important, from a self-care perspective and from a consent culture perspective, to remember that they are going at their own pace. They are on their own journeys and so are you. Anything you share, share from a place of care, hope, and personal experience, rather than prescriptiveness! If you are trying to keep up, remember that those guiding you also stumbled and fell, and still do. Things don't change overnight, and one person can't typically change another person's mind, but minds and behaviors do often shift thanks to role modeling. Be patient with yourself and with those around you!

....

Prompt: This may have been a really intense process for you, so congratulations for getting here! What are some techniques in your toolkit for taking better care of yourself and your boundaries that you've found useful during this process? What are some new ones that you may pick up to try to help you recharge?

DAY TWENTY-TWO: HOW ARE YOU DOING?

Day Twenty-Three:
How Can You Empower Yourself
to Act in Support of Others?

An obstacle to communities feeling safe is whether members feel they have a voice when something goes sideways. Sometimes the barrier to feeling like you have a voice comes from within and your own confidence, and sometimes, it comes from the ways in which the community organizes and handles itself. There are lots of ways we can educate ourselves and structure our communities to foster compassionate accountability. Some of them are outlined in the resources at the back of this book, and I hope you'll check them out!

Here's a reflection from my own past:

> When I first launched the consent culture workshop Safe/Ward, I had worked on creating a bunch of solutions for issues I saw standing in the way of an environment centered around consent in kink spaces. I had considered lighting, how loud the music was, the diversity and accessibility of the hosts, and transparency around what the accountability process looked like. I knew I didn't want to offer complaints without proposed ways to move forward and make improvements, so I poured my energy into ensuring I had ideas.
>
> What I didn't realize was that my ideas would not be taken as a jumping-off point for others to

come up with their own that would best fit their community needs. Instead, I had emails pouring in from people who wanted me to offer my judgment and answer to their very specific situations. People wanted me to be the judge and jury for their conflicts, and as a woman in my twenties, I was absolutely overwhelmed. I wanted to help, I didn't want to blow these people off or ignore them, but I was also drowning under the tsunami of pleas, and I was neglecting my own needs in the process.

I ended up coming up with a few solutions to help me help others while also taking care of myself. First, I wrote a few community guides to help people make their own decisions based on the variety of possibilities I had presented in my workshops. This encouraged people to build on my work, which took a large load off my shoulders.

I also gently but firmly began to request that communities needing more support actually pay me for consultation and training. I came up with some payment options and cost-effective ways to do the consultations, but I made sure that if I was putting in more than fifteen minutes helping a community I was not actively involved in, I was getting paid.

It felt extremely uncomfortable, like I was putting my activism behind a paywall. I soon saw that doing this both cut down on the demands for my time, and that when communities paid me for my expertise, they were a lot more likely to listen and take my advice on board.

I know that I have a lot of experience and skill sets that make me a valuable asset in figuring out healthier community dynamics. I know I can support others both as a teacher and as a platform raising other people up as leaders. I now know that doing those things takes a lot of emotional energy, and that emotional energy is finite. If I spend it on activism, I don't have it to spend on my work or my own community. Asking to be paid for that time and effort is a solution that makes it sustainable for me.

If I were to choose one of my central pieces of advice, it would be this: When it comes to empowering yourself as a supporter, it is useful to learn about bystander intervention, basic first-responder protocol for victims of violence, and de-escalation techniques. Knowing how to respond to situations without defensiveness is a skill that you have to practice to improve. You will likely still feel nervous when you suddenly need to put those techniques into action, but you will feel more prepared and capable because you have a program in your head that you can use as a guide. This kind of education will also help you recognize your own emotional and physical needs and separate them from the emotional and physical needs radiating off someone in crisis, which can help both of your needs be better communicated and met.

Many situations involving accountability are not crisis situations. That said, knowing how to respond if you *do* encounter a crisis situation means you won't feel unprepared if someone comes to you with a traumatic experience.

....

Prompt: What's a way that you, as an individual, could support others in situations where they are seeking account-ability and/or community support? What kind of support do you need for that to feel safe? How can you preemptively request that support?

Day Twenty-Four:
How Can You Be Accountable?

It took me an embarrassingly long time to reprogram myself out of being defensive when someone told me I had hurt them in some way. I didn't *mean* to, I'd say, or I didn't know that what I did was hurtful—as if that took the effects of my actions away or gave solace to the person I affected. Sometimes I found ways to directly or indirectly blame the other person for their feelings, like it was a communication issue on their part, or they took what I did too personally.

Leslee Petersen, activist for LGBTQ+ and polyamorous rights and ex-libertarian, writes:

> My husband and I have a partner who, many years ago, lived an hour away from us. We would regularly visit him and he would visit us.
>
> After a time in which my husband and I were going through family deaths, we started becoming lax in consideration for our other partner. We would often show up late for dinners and sometimes without a call. Our comfort with our partner led to an assumption that he would be comfortable with our lateness. He was not. He was hurt by our lack of respect for his time by being routinely late. One day, visibly hurt, he gave us an ultimatum that we needed to respect his time or we would have to end

our relationship. My husband and I were shocked! We didn't think that it had been an issue. We apologized, profusely. But then we also started giving excuses. We were busy, we were stressed, it was a long drive, something unexpected, etc. To us they were reasons, explanations. To our partner they said that we placed ourselves above taking the time to plan for the emergencies. It was clear the damage had been done.

Over the next year, my husband and I made an effort to be on time or early whenever we would see our partner. Our actions spoke louder than our words and our relationship was repaired. We valued our partner and that he had trusted us enough to set a boundary, and we valued him enough to change our behavior.

I wish that I hadn't felt the need to explain and dismiss his hurt. My reasons for being late were not emergencies or crises that were unavoidable, it was simply a matter of disregard and assumption it would be fine. Over the years I've grown to sit with the feelings of defensiveness when I'm told I have hurt someone, and I credit this instance with being a learning experience. Now, I listen fully to the person expressing their feelings and apologize immediately. I make mental notes that my excuses are not part of this conversation and let my mind run through them to completion before I come back and offer solutions for rectification.

Thankfully my husband, partner, and I all live in the same town now, and it makes life so much easier! The three of us have meals together, watch movies, or just hang out chatting for hours and hours. We had, and still have, a comfortable relationship and have grown together through ups and downs over almost a decade together.

It took me a lot of introspection and humility, but now I understand that my knee-jerk reaction to being told I hurt someone is feeling guilty and ashamed, and that my defensiveness is a natural self-protection response. That said, just because something comes to us automatically doesn't mean that it's the right thing to do. I have absolutely kicked a table leg after stubbing my toe on it because striking out was my automatic response to the pain. It didn't help matters. My toe was just twice stubbed. I realized that it was perhaps in my best interest to explore my reactions and see if they were actually useful to me or standing in my way.

I also realize now that when someone offers me feedback or criticism about my behavior, I don't have to receive it as an attack. Our society tends to make these situations combative, but as Dungeons and Dragons has taught me, just because the game pushes you toward fighting your problems away, doesn't mean there aren't other, better, more appropriate methods.

Now, when someone tells me I hurt them, I can feel the anxiety pang in my stomach and the flush of shame in my cheeks, *and I can stop myself.* I can breathe through it, remind myself that I am not in danger and that I don't need to be hypervigilant, that this person is telling me this so that I can improve myself and thus not hurt people in the future, which is a gift. I can stay calm and apologize, and I can ask what I can do to fix it, if I can fix it. Later, I can reflect on the situation further—I can consider the context in which the feedback was given, my history with that person, and if I can see where they were coming from. And I'll be honest—sometimes, I genuinely can't. After all, not all feedback is given in good faith. But if I don't react defensively, if I choose to react as if it *is* being given in good faith and receive it as such, it will empower a person who really is hurt and will disempower someone trying to get a reaction out of me. Either way, the result is better than a defensive response would have gotten.

....

Prompt: Think back to a time someone told you that you hurt them. How did you react? Why do you think you reacted that way? After working through some of the questions and reading some of the stories in this book, how would you like to react now? What are some ways you can self-regulate to better be present and open to feedback?

Day Twenty-Five:
What Are Some Small
Steps You Can Take?

It's easy to get lost in all the huge changes that need to happen for our world to be healthier and more sustainable, both for the planet and for humanity. As someone who was writing furious letters to the president about climate change and protecting abortion clinics from angry protesters when I was a child, I have felt weighed down by all the shifts I feel need to happen. Sometimes I feel small and lost under the vastness of what needs to be done. I wonder what real difference I, just one person, can really make.

As an adult, though, I've witnessed that one person can spark change. When I started the Consent Culture Project, people were mostly just talking about how to avoid rape culture, not what we wanted to see instead. I bounced off a couple of other people who were also interested in that discussion, and our ideas, written in our small, niche blogs, began to get news coverage and attention.

It's not just activism for which this is true, either. When I first moved to the Bay Area, everyone *hugged* me. They didn't ask, they just said they were huggers and went for it. I felt like a strangled feral cat, and didn't know how to resist, so I just felt uncomfortable for the first year. But then, I began to respond differently. When they said "Oh, I'm a hugger," I immediately took a step back, one hand between me and the other person, a smile on my face, and said "That's great! I'm not, but it's nice to meet you." It took a bit, but establishing my boundary in this way, consistently, was a small step that ended up having bigger ramifications—now, people in many of the spaces I'm in ask whether I would like a hug before stepping in for one, and I feel so much more comfortable. Considering the number of people who have thanked me for doing this, it seems asserting my autonomy also helped them assert theirs!

One person, it turns out, can encourage a small group, who then encourage a community, who then encourage the world.

Shane Burley, editor of *Why We Fight: Essays on Fascism, Resistance, and Surviving the Apocalypse*, writes:

> Making the case for consent is easy. I could quote the growing body of literature, cite from presentations and workshops, even provide a few choice personal examples I am proud of. But this negates one uncomfortable reality: men are bad at consent, and that means all of us. Male sociability is grounded in breaking through the barriers that consent creates because, only then, can we remain competitive in a world designed for conquest rather than collaboration and kindness. I first took a consent workshop at twenty-seven years old, two decades past when I should have. It would be a farce to present myself as anything other than a person struggling with how to consent better each day.
>
> "Asking means preparing yourself for no," is something I've heard my wife say a lot over our near decade together. The withholding of consent depends on a certain covenant that should occur

between two people. One person says what they want, and the other person has to listen to know. This caused some of the most profound breaks in my own relationship, ones that, as time has gone on, I feel like I have only gotten a handle on more recently.

Part of the challenges I have had with my spouse is being able to really hear what she is asking of me instead of just projecting my own feelings onto her. When she first used the term gaslighting, I didn't know what it meant (I thought it meant throwing gas on the fire, like making someone intentionally angry), but even after I had read two dozen articles and had even more conversations about the subject, I still couldn't locate it. When accused of it, I ducked out, thinking my own feelings of hurt inoculated me from my ability to be abusive.

There is a difference between what happens in a person's interior life and what goes on outside them. It may seem obvious, but it is hardly subjectively so, and this created a fog that escalated conflicts as I deflected, diverted, and refused responsibility, even when it was glaringly obvious. In one particular argument, my wife put forward something hurtful I had said, and she asked why. "That's not what I meant. You said something really similar. Why is that what you focus on rather than all the wonderful things I've done?" I responded. It was only when I finally froze, listened, and refused to simply "react" that I realized that what I had done was still there, and no amount of negotiating had changed it.

The steps necessary to make this change seem mundane and obvious, but they were like a sea change. They began with committing to simply believing what I am told, that someone's hurt is their own and honestly shared, and that what was being requested was intentional. There is a brokenness that pushes people to assume bad-faith attacks even at the most crucial points of vulnerability, so when someone expresses their hurt to you, your belief in them mirrors that vulnerability. The next step was to listen and act based on what I was told, not simply as the result of stories I had written and replayed about what happened. To repair and grow you have to have internalized what changes are necessary— it's the first step to building a plan for those shifts. This required a great deal of faith, mostly in my own ability to do what felt like moving mountains, to unlearn responses that failed to serve me or anyone in my life.

In a brusque conversation one day, my wife, after a breathy pause, told me that my dismissive tone hurt her and made her feel small. When someone confronts you with your behavior, it can be jarring since, presumably, you did not actively intend to make them feel bad. I stopped, listened, and immediately validated the experience, saying that I would learn from this situation so that I could try to approach communications with more intentional care. These are the kind of conversations that are now common, where both of us intervene if some-one feels off, and we expect the other to listen and to believe.

This is no magic realization—it is just one of many that, hopefully, makes up the growth I'm trying to make. But it necessarily means that I have to, essen-tially, sit with my brokenness. To hear someone else means a willingness to change, and that means the ability to expose and clean your wounds. To make hearing successful, you have to be willing to shed the trumped-up image of who you want to be and learn to sit with who you actually are. But what does it mean to be accountable to that? Are we open about our failures?

Early Hasidic leader Rabbi Menachem Mendel of Kotzk wrote that "there is nothing so whole as a broken heart." Rabbi Mendel, who would spark a dynastic movement still around today, echoed the creation story found in the Kabbalah of Isaac Luria, which is a form of Jewish mysticism that set the stage for most later movements looking to understand the nature of G-d in Judaism. Luria had to reconcile something: G-d's oneness with our profound brokenness. He did this by explaining that G-d shattered themself when making the universe, scattering the broken pieces. Brokenness is where we started. There was nothing before.

There is something freeing about acknowledging we were broken from the start. Luria's answer to brokenness was not despair, but to gush with love. By engaging in the ritual work of Tikkun Olam, the healing of the world, we bring those pieces back together, we build something a little less imperfect than what we started with. Judaism has its own unique relationship to the balance of perfection and imperfection. The pagans saw the world as inherently sacred, while the Christians saw it as base and profane (so we must escape). Jews had a different intervention: it was profane, to be made holy. Each day we look at how to intervene in the mundanity and build the sacred. The spark only exists in our choices, the Kavvanah (inner intentions), and the real-world actions we take. Our hearts aren't enough. Our actions (however small) matter.

To do this is to treat each moment as the first. The ability for us to make a change, to see our failures, and to learn to really see another person, is one we have at each instant. This is where the real danger lies, in risking the safety of the "craven images" we have about ourselves, the stories we tell to absolve our responsibility. There is a victory in acknowledging that we aren't who we want to be because that's the only way becoming something else is possible.

For consent to be a standard, we have to engage in healing. Not the commercial type of self-care, full of affirmations and euphoric delusions, but the kind of healing that hurts, that requires something of us, that has weight and consequences and the risk of loss. But when you open yourself up to really hearing another person, you find out that you share a broken heart, and that vulnerability is a new kind of world. Sitting with that vulnerability is a small step we can take, that we have control over, that can make a world of difference.

I'm a big proponent of making small but significant changes by changing my own behavior in the hopes that other people will see it and model their own after it. One of the main ways I do that in my day to day is by remembering that I can't necessarily heal the entire world, but I can shift the way people who encounter me today think about their own autonomy and consent. I can't do everything, but I can do *something*, and that's a start.

When we started Kinky Salon London, we had a theme planned called Jungle Bonk. My co-founder, Tobias, and I thought, how fun, a rainforest type of theme feels lush and exciting, and as we both loved Disney, why not reference *The Jungle Book*? We hadn't considered, from our positions of white privilege and well-meaning ignorance, that Rudyard Kipling was a massive racist, that it was highly suspect to throw a party with such a theme when the community was mostly white Londoners, and that it opened the door to some gross colonialism and exoticism of the South Asian members in our group.

So, when we announced the theme, some people understandably threatened to picket the event. I remember realizing that we had fucked up, and that these people were right. Rather than get defensive or double down, I reached out, apologized, and asked what we could do to fix the situation. We ended up making a public statement, changing the theme to Ecosexual (which carried none of the same implications), and listening to the marginalized members of our community. Several of the people who were ready to condemn us are now some of my closest friends, in part because I trust them to be honest with me.

This example of accountability is a small thing in the scope of the world issues we have at hand. But it ended up having a rippling effect, not just in my personal life, but in the larger scope of how people in the Kinky Salon London community threw parties and listened to their communities. It opened a wider discussion about othering and parties, and how to be more conscious about it. By focusing on a small thing I could personally do to encourage a more accountable consent culture in a space where I had influence, I effected more change than I ever would have thought.

Not that there are laurels to rest on, either—allyship is, as Mia McKenzie of Black Girl Dangerous says, not an identity but a practice. It is a muscle we can and should exercise every day, in ways that allow us to build up muscle tone and keep ourselves stronger. It's important to be consistent and sustainable in our goals, because that creates a stable, reliable foundation on which we can build. By modeling the behaviors we want to see, we can create the consent culture we want to live in.

....

Prompt: While it's easy to be caught up in desires for big changes, it's important to look at the little, achievable actions we can do to move toward the world we want to see. What is something you can do tomorrow to encourage a consent culture in your life?

Day Twenty-Six:
How Can We Pass Along
What We've Learned?

When I was growing up, consent wasn't really a thing we were encouraged to teach kids. We knew to report "bad touches," but we were also told to respect authority and that adults were always right. Thankfully, I was raised by parents who encouraged me to have bodily autonomy and the language to define it, but I knew I was on the fringe even as a teenager.

Teaching children about consent has gained increasing attention over the years, particularly when it comes to things like unwanted hugs or respecting boundaries around tickling. We are beginning to understand that the ways in which we talk about and advocate for boundaries and consent in our interactions with children make a deep impression on them and help them feel increased bodily autonomy.

Jenny Wilson, founder of ConsentCulture.co.uk and creator of the International Day of Consent, writes:

> Consent is about choices, agreements, permission. Consent culture is about living in a way that supports and encourages agency, autonomy, and intentional ways of relating. These aren't complicated ideas, but high-profile debate around sexual consent has formed an association that makes consent an awkward topic for some people.

Talking with children about sex involves responding to their natural curiosity with honesty and openness in an age-appropriate way. In my experience, being matter of fact about sex means discussing it like any other natural behaviour. Being open and not shrouding sex in euphemism and shame means young people can feel able to speak openly about issues or worries, and this in turn supports safeguarding.

When we approach consent more broadly, as part of all our interactions, not just the intimate and private ones, then even really young kids can understand, express, and navigate it. If we want children to develop confidence about communicating and respecting agency, autonomy, and boundaries, I think the most powerful way to teach that is by modeling consent—showing children that we respect them and expecting the same from them toward us and each other.

When we change a baby's nappy, we can treat them like an object that needs cleaning or we can make eye contact, talk, and treat their body respectfully. When a small child says they don't like tickling games, we can ignore them and play on, or we can listen and stop. When one kid loves to hug and their pal hates hugs, we can show them both how to ask, and how to say and hear "no." These learning opportunities happen every day.

It's not just kids who need to learn about consent, though. Many elders associate consent with sex, which can sometimes load a conversation about it with awkwardness or shame. We might not even bother to try. We might dismiss older people as less enlightened because they grew up in a less progressive time. We might excuse older people's unhealthy consent practices because "it was different in their day." The idea of respecting your elders can come with a whiff of condescension, talking down to the "old dear." Elderly people are all too often treated like they have less capacity to consent. Assuming that aging means becoming physically and/or mentally infirm leads to treating elders with reduced agency. None of this is OK. It doesn't communicate or model consent.

When a kid doesn't want to kiss their grandma, we can cajole or coerce them into it, or we can support them to find another way to show affection, at the same time showing grandma how we respect boundaries. Modeling consent is a way to demonstrate consent culture to people of any age. Consent conversations work well if they're about something that's relatable and fairly easy to talk about, like respecting each other's space.

It's usually a good idea to challenge assumptions if you want to be more consensual and that includes assumptions about age and capacity to consent. Communicating with curiosity and empathy can help us all find common ground and ways to connect within consent.

Interestingly, it's in these discussions around teaching children that I see people really grasping that consent is about more than sexuality. Knowing and communicating your limits around nonsexual touch impacts us in many areas of our lives, including at the doctor, at school, or on the playground, and having the language and confidence to assert those boundaries can help us when it comes to dealing with creepy behavior.

We encourage children to tell someone they trust if they feel their boundaries have been crossed. Why, then, do we penalize people for talking about abuse and assault as adults? What do children learn when they see celebrities come forward about their experiences only to be dragged and insulted by the media? How could we be more consistent in our messaging?

Additionally, one area I'd love to see consent educators and advocates talking more about is consent with the elderly. Most of the articles I see around the topic revolve around dementia and sexual consent, an interesting and important aspect and one I'm not qualified to discuss in detail, but it's also certainly not the only one. Legal consent, medical consent, asking before moving someone's body to shift them onto a bed or before touching their arm to steady them— these are all consent issues that can help someone who may feel disempowered gain some sense of autonomy. After all, not all elderly people are disabled, and many disabled people who aren't elderly struggle with these issues too.

Other generations have different language around consent—what I might call getting consent before using someone's first name, my grandmother would have simply called good manners. Just as with children, I think it's useful to consider mirroring language when discussing consent with elders. The active listening skills that enable you to speak on the same level will also encourage trust, which makes space to ask questions and gain better understanding.

Talking to our elders about consent as it pertains to their bodily autonomy when receiving medical or personal care is equally as important in my mind as how to communicate these issues to our children. Thinking about how we can meet people where they're at, not just in our generation but in the ones before and after us, encourages us to critically think about consent from other perspectives.

....

Prompt: It is vital to learn how to talk about big topics like consent culture in different ways for different audiences, particularly across generational divides. How might you break down the idea of consent to a small child? How would you describe consent culture to an elder?

Day Twenty-Seven:
Can We Take a Moment
for Self-Reflection?

I have a tattoo on my arm that says "evolve or die." It seems aggressive, but I don't have it as a demand for other people—it's a reminder to myself that adaptation is the best way to survive, and that without growth and change we grow stagnant, wither, and "die." I am a product of the choices I make and the communities I touch, a constantly updating software that seeks to improve upon itself.

It's kind of funny—working on writing this workbook ended up being a way for me to go through all these prompts myself and reflect on the long history I've had with consent culture. I've been doing this work for over ten years, and I'm still defining what a consent culture is and what it could look like. I've even learned a few things, especially as I went back and read my own earlier writings on consent—and I literally wrote the book!

Writing this workbook showed me how much I've changed, from my teenage years to my twenties to now. I put a lot of pressure on myself to uncover the One Right Answer. I used to feel that consent was cut and dry, black and white, something that we could develop a formula for that would ensure every interaction was enthusiastically consensual.

That's a good ideal to have, certainly, but as I've gotten older I've begun to realize how unrealistic that is. It's not just because of human nature and our individual needs to be more enlightened. It's also something that needs to be tackled at an institutional level before many of us are able to embody a consent culture as individuals.

Perhaps because I've become more forgiving of myself and my own fallibility, I have also developed more compassion to others struggling to find their footholds. I'm not as quick to condemn as I once was. I still believe that there are people who demonstrate a complete lack of desire to be a respectful member of society and who are not mindful of others' boundaries, and I do think that consequences sometimes need to be harsh to show that a behavior pattern is unacceptable and will not be tolerated. But I've also learned that many times boundary violations are far more complex than simply "this person is evil and cruel." I now take power dynamics, histories of behavior, communication styles, environment, and culture into account. The more I study consent culture, the more I realize I have much to learn.

Perhaps a consent culture is not a concrete thing, but a conversation we are having, continually, within ourselves and with each other. Maybe perfection isn't achievable and that's OK. Maybe the best thing we can do is learn to accept accountability with humility and grace. Seems like as good a place as any to start.

....

Prompt: What is something you've learned about yourself while going through the questions in this book? What's something you feel confident you have a handle on, and what's something you'd like to develop further?

Day Twenty-Eight:
What Is Consent Culture?

I've offered up anecdotes, both my own and other people's, throughout this workbook so that you can see the ways in which we agree and the ways in which we differ. I don't know of just one immutable definition of what consent culture is. It evolves with us.

I hope you have found this workbook helpful, and that it being broken down into bite-sized pieces helped you work through the information. I know consent is a huge topic, and this is just a starting place. I wanted to conclude with a question that gets you to explore how you would define consent culture now that you've done some introspection and thought critically about the influences we have in our lives. Maybe your answer will be the same as when you started this journey, or maybe it will have expanded, changed, or grown in new ways.

Our time together is coming to a close, and so I'll end with this wish for you: May accountability increasingly feel like a blessing in your life, not a curse.

....

Prompt: How would you define a consent culture after going through the questions in this book? How has your understanding of consent stayed the same? Did it expand or become more defined? In what ways?

The End Is Just the Beginning

*The world should have protected you, but you have
been asked to protect it. What an honor. What
an injustice.*

—Brian Murphy, *Not Another D&D Podcast*

I originally put together *Ask: Building Consent Culture* to
signal-boost marginalized voices talking about the myriad of
ways that coercion and consent violations impact our day-
to-day lives and to encourage the reader to ask questions
about why that's the case. I wanted to push back against the
way that consent had been boiled down to focus only on heterosexual sexual assault. I wanted to smash the ivory tower
where people were deciding what consent conversations
were important. I wanted to platform people who experience
institutional violence that infringes on their consent on a
daily basis.

With this workbook, I decided to ask the questions myself,
and to ask them of you. Just as with my first book, I didn't
want to lie and say I have the answers—I don't. But I did want
to offer some guiding questions to help you stretch your critical thinking muscles and come to your own conclusions.

Even so, I didn't want you to feel abandoned. These are
intense, deep questions, and trying to answer them can feel
overwhelming. I think we each ask ourselves, "who am I to say?"
when it comes to solving big social issues, and there's a humility

to be found in that. Indeed, who are you and who am I? We are all just wounded animals stumbling through the brush.

It was important to me to use this workbook as another opportunity to open the scope of the questions and whose voices we get to hear. I hope I offered you a helpful variety of experiences in the anecdotes I curated. I wanted to reassure you that community leaders, sex educators, and therapists don't have The Answer, either. We just have more questions leading us toward improving our relationship to consent. And that's OK.

It was also really important to me that the language of this workbook be accessible and inviting. I know I can be kind of an intense person! I didn't want this to use academic language or a bunch of citations you needed to look up. I wanted to provide resources to help guide you forward and a glossary for how I use the terms I use in here, but I didn't want this to feel like classwork. I hope you have found the prompts and anecdotes here to be gentle, rather than gatekeeping or alientating, and that they invited you to explore your beliefs and experiences through a new lens. I want you to leave this work feeling curious, not lectured.

I know doing the work to understand what consent and consent culture mean to you personally can be hard and humbling. Nothing has shown me how little I knew about myself and how much I assumed and took for granted about my experience being universal like talking about consent culture! It can sometimes feel embarrassing to realize the limitations of my scope or uncomfortable to realize that something I had blown off as no big deal was, in fact, important.

I believe that learning what you don't know is something powerful and beautiful. When you understand what you have left to learn, you can begin to develop those skills. You can become better informed, and your consent can become more finely tuned. And the more you uncover, the more compassionate you can be for others and their journeys, while also maintaining the boundaries you need to feel secure.

Of course, it's not just about the boundaries themselves, or communicating consent before the fact. My hope is that you will have learned how to be accountable in ways that hurt you and those around you less. Like a clown learning to take a fall, with more practice and introspection, I hope you will be able to take ownership with more grace, which will help those around you to feel safer talking to you. Consent culture is a mutual aid effort, and our individual work can spread to those around us like wildflowers from a seed bomb.

I believe strongly that people mostly don't come into the world wanting to hurt each other. They become traumatized and scared and lash out, they learn it's effective, and they cycle when traumatized again. "Hurt people hurt people," as the saying goes. Having compassion for people's processes doesn't mean putting up with bullshit, though. I think it's useful to understand, for your own knowledge and for those around you, that not all coping mechanisms are good or healthy, even if they are understandable.

Boundaries don't have to be walls, and they don't have to be permanent, but they can become that way if a more flexible fence doesn't suffice. While I believe strongly that most people want to learn and evolve and grow, we must understand that we are not entitled to someone walking alongside us during that process. I think this is important to remember when we're figuring out our own boundaries around a toxic situation, that we are allowed to walk away if we need to or want to. It's also important when we're the ones doing the lashing out and we find ourselves on our own. People who stick with us and yet hold us accountable while we evolve are gifts to be valued, not something we are entitled to.

I think most people really do want to do better and be better. They just need a little help figuring out the tools. I hope this workbook was a helpful tool for you in grappling with the complexity that is consent, and I hope you carry that work forward into your life. Modeling is one of the most effective ways to effect change.

I believe that building a consent culture and thinking critically about what that actually means in practice will help us not only hurt each other less but also hurt ourselves less. I know in my heart that we absolutely must address and abolish predatory power structures to have a chance in hell of giving and receiving true consent. This is a living document, and a process. May we always be growing.

I believe in you. I believe in us.

Resources

Note: I personally do not agree with everything presented in all of these books, but I still think they are useful in helping people think critically about the topic at hand. Some are about community activism, some are about romantic relationships, and some are about introspective work on your own boundaries. I think there's something to gain in them all, and they've all informed my beliefs. And there's much more out there!

Books/Essays

- *Beyond Survival: Strategies and Stories from the Transformative Justice Movement*, edited by Leah Lakshmi Piepzna-Samarasinha and Ejeris Dixon
- *Can I Give You a Squish?* by Emily Neilson
- *Can We Talk About Consent?: A Book About Freedom, Choices, and Agreement* by Justin Hancock and Fuchsia MacAree
- *Conflict Is Not Abuse: Overstating Harm, Community Responsibility, and the Duty of Repair* by Sarah Schulman
- *Consent (for Kids!): Boundaries, Respect, and Being in Charge of YOU* by Rachel Brian
- *Difficult Conversations: How to Discuss What Matters Most* by Douglas Stone, Bruce Patton, and Sheila Heen
- *Disrupting the Bystander: When #MeToo Happens Among Friends* by A.V. Flox
- *Energetic Boundaries: How to Stay Protected and Connected in Work, Love, and Life* by Cyndi Dale
- *From White Racist to White Anti-Racist: The Life-Long Journey* by Tema Okun
- *Fumbling Towards Repair: A Workbook for Community Accountability Facilitators* by Mariame Kaba and Shira Hassan

- *Hegemony How-To: A Road Map for Radicals* by Jonathan Smucker
- *I Never Called It Rape: The Ms. Report on Recognizing, Fighting, and Surviving Date and Acquaintance Rape* by Robin Warshaw
- *Learning Good Consent: Building Ethical Relationships in a Complicated World*, edited by Cindy Crabb
- *Love's Not Color Blind: Race and Representation in Polyamorous and Other Alternative Communities* by Kevin A. Patterson, foreword by Ruby Bouie Johnson
- *Pleasure Activism: The Politics of Feeling Good* by adrienne maree brown
- *Polysecure: Attachment, Trauma and Consensual Nonmonogamy* by Jessica Fern, foreword by Eve Rickert and Nora Samaran
- *Sexual Revolution: Modern Fascism and the Feminist Fightback* by Laurie Penny
- *So You Want to Talk About Race* by Ijeoma Oluo
- *Speaking from the Heart: 18 Languages for Modern Love* by Anne Hodder-Shipp
- *The Art of Receiving and Giving: The Wheel of Consent* by Betty Martin with Robyn Dalzen
- *The Body Is Not an Apology: The Power of Radical Self-Love* by Sonya Renee Taylor
- *The Five Love Languages: How to Express Heartfelt Commitment to Your Mate* by Gary Chapman
- *The Revolution Starts at Home: Confronting Intimate Violence Within Activist Communities*, edited by Ching-In Chen, Jai Dulani, and Leah Lakshmi Piepzna-Samarasinha
- *Tomorrow Sex Will Be Good Again: Women and Desire in the Age of Consent* by Katherine Angel
- *Unfuck Your Boundaries: Build Better Relationships Through Consent, Communication, and Expressing Your Needs* by Faith G. Harper
- *We Do This 'Til We Free Us: Abolitionist Organizing and Transforming Justice* by Mariame Kaba, edited by Tamara K. Nopper, foreword by Naomi Murakawa
- *Yes Means Yes!: Visions of Female Sexual Power and a World Without Rape*, edited by Jaclyn Friedman and Jessica Valenti

Websites

- Captain Awkward: excellent advice on communication and boundary setting. captainawkward.com
- Consent Culture US: the website I created to set the tone of what consent culture means and how to work toward it. consentculture.com
- Consent Culture UK: the website created by Jenny Wilson toward building a culture of consent through campaigns, resources, and arts and cultural interventions. consentculture.co.uk
- INCITE!: radical feminists of color organizing around ending state violence in their communities and offering thorough resources on community accountability. incite-national.org
- International Day of Consent (#IDoConsent, November 30). idoconsent.org
- Make It About Race!: an intersectional approach to teaching about consent by Dr. Nadine Thornhill. nadinethornhill.com/make-it-about-race
- Nurturing Human Touch: a starting place for exploring consent and touch. nurturinghumantouch.com
- Tits and Sass: writing by sex workers for sex workers about topics like survival sex work, disability, and sex work in a pandemic. titsandsass.com
- YourTripSister: responsible psychedelic use and education. yourtripsister.com

Podcasts

- *American Sex Podcast*: an AASECT award-winning podcast hosted by Sunny Megatron and dedicated to changing America's dysfunctional relationship with sex. americansexpodcast.com
- *The Ex-Worker*: an anarchist podcast dealing with various ideas and actions. This episode is specifically about community accountability. crimethinc.com/podcasts/the-ex-worker/episodes/8

- *Glow West*: a podcast that explores sex, sexuality, and the body from a sexual wellness perspective, hosted by Dr. Caroline West. glowwest.org
- *Non-Monogamy Help*: a relationship advice podcast for people in nonmonogamous or polyamorous relationships, hosted by Lola Phoenix. nonmonogamyhelp.com
- *Unlocking Us*: a podcast about deeply personal topics, including shame, accountability, vulnerability, and more, hosted by NYT bestseller Brené Brown. brenebrown.com/podcast/ brene-on-shame-and-accountability

Crisis Resources

- First Response to Sexual Assault: a flyer with good advice if you find yourself as the first point of contact with a sexual assault survivor. tinyurl.com/305lvan
- Kink Aware Professionals: therapists, doctors, and other professionals who have experience with alternative relationships, organized by the National Coalition for Sexual Freedom. kapprofessionals.org
- National Domestic Violence Hotline: a 24/7 hotline with an extensive resource list organized by state. 1-800-799-SAFE (7233) or TTY 1-800-787-3224, thehotline.org
- Gay Men's Domestic Violence Project: a 24/7 hotline that supports victims and survivors through education, advocacy, and direct services. 1-800-832-1901
- RAINN: Rape, Abuse and Incest National Network – trained staff members offering confidential crisis support. 1-800-656-HOPE (4673), hotline.rainn.org/online
- Trans Lifeline: trans peer support hotline by and for trans folks. US: 1-877-565-8860, Canada: 1-877-330-6366, translifeline.org
- The Trevor Project: free, trained crisis counselors focused on LGBTQ+ youth. 1-866-488-7386, thetrevorproject.org/get-help

Contributors

Angelique Luna is a pleasure-focused psychic. Using her experience as a certified kink-aware and conscious erotic touch professional along with her intuitive psychic medium skills, she makes it easy to talk about taboo topics.

Avens O'Brien is a speaker, writer, and advocate for her vision of a peaceful, voluntary world where consent culture is applied to all things. She's a board member of Feminists for Liberty, libertarian activist, an entrepreneur and educator in psychedelic spaces, and a lover of birds. Her project @YourTripSister seeks to educate users of maximum enjoyment and risk reduction when using common psychedelics.

Epiphany Jordan has been providing, researching, writing about, and thinking about human touch for the past ten years. She is the author of *Somebody Hold Me: The Single Person's Guide to Nurturing Human Touch*, and the founder of Karuna Sessions, a service that provides platonic touch in a ritualized setting. She is currently working on an MPH in Social Marketing from the University of South Florida and wants to create public-health programs that use nurturing human touch as a wellness practice. She lives in Reno, Nevada, with her floor dragons, Stormy and Hoover. nurturinghumantouch.com.

Intimacy ConAmore is a multiracial Two-Spirit Afab Indigenous Native American Black person who is polyamorous, kinky, Demisexual/Asexual Bisexual/Pansexual and Solopoly but open to all humans, not based on gender, sexuality, or genitalia. They are the mom of two young Black men and grew up with polyamorous swinger grandparents — their grandmother taught them all about swinger etiquette! Intimacy is into unfiltered authenticity of self and uninhibited connectivity with others. A polyamorous veteran of over thirty years, they have hosted events since 2014 to advocate, educate, and support polyamorous communities. They have presented at multiple polyamorous-focused conferences and other events. They also work in the human sexuality fields of education and services as a $exy surrogate, compassionate companion, and a sensuality self-love mentor.

Jenny Wilson instigated the International Day of Consent (November 30) in 2018 and champions consent culture via performances, writing, workshops, rituals, discussions, podcasts, and festivals. Based in Bradford, UK, she founded Irregular Arts from a belief that the arts can engage, challenge, delight, and make change. She performs character-based work, including gender-queer drag character Mysti Valentine, in cabaret, festivals, live art, and street performance. Queer, neurodivergent, relationship anarchist, and a solo parent, Jenny is also in Activist Residency at Leeds Beckett University Psychology Deptartment sssH! Stigmatised Sexualities and Sexual Harm Research Group. She is also the chair of Happy Valley Pride, a coach, a restorative practitioner, and a facilitator. consentculture.co.uk and loveoffscript.co.uk.

Kitty Stryker has been working on defining and creating a consent culture for over ten years through her writing, workshops, and website. She's the editor of *Ask: Building Consent Culture,* and is especially interested in bringing conversations about consent out of the bedroom and into everyday life. Additionally, Kitty is a sex worker and academic on the history of obscenity, censorship, and queer culture. In her copious free time, Kitty enjoys working as a street medic for direct actions, playing Dungeons and Dragons, and indulging her two cats. She's considering going back to school to explore the intersection of consent and law. She identifies as a queer, asexual, sober, anarchist, and femme. consentculture.com and @kittystryker.

Kori Doty is a genderqueer community educator based on Lekwungan Territory on the island colonially known as Vancouver Island. They have worked in sexual health, harm reduction, and community wellness education for over ten years and are now expanding their skills and knowledge within somatic practices towards liberation through embodiment. They host the monthly online event the Sex Toy Show & Tell and the podcast *Imagination Revolution: UBI.* They also write a blog and their work has been included in anthologies and collections including the 2022 co-edited title *The Liminal Chrysalis: Imagining Reproduction and Parenting Futures Beyond the Binary.* koridoty.com.

Leslee Petersen was a decade-long activist in the libertarian community. They have recently left that space. Their activism focused on queer and polyamorous rights, social justice, and consent. They live in New Hampshire with their partners, cats, and snakes.

Nazelah Jamison is a Bay Area–based performance poet, author, actor, vocalist, and emcee. Her first book of poetry, *Evolutionary Heart,* was released by Nomadic Press in 2016. Her work can also be found in *Culture Counts Magazine,*

The Racket Journal, and other publications. In her spare time, Nazelah enjoys writing horror screenplays and saving the day. She hosts the Nomadic Press Virtual Open Mic every Friday and gives the best hugs in the Bay Area.

Pete Bailey is a gay rights activist, erotica and memoir writer, doodler, former sex worker, and current mental health occupational therapist. He uses images and stories as tools to share his experiences and facilitate others to share their stories. He is the co-editor of *Trans Homo... Gasp!,* which was nominated for a Lambda Literary Award.

Shane Burley is a journalist based in Portland, Oregon, who primarily covers social movements. He authored *Why We Fight: Essays on Fascism, Resistance, and Surviving the Apocalypse* (AK Press, 2021) and *Fascism Today: What It Is and How to End It* (AK Press, 2017). He is also the editor of the forthcoming anthology *¡No pasarán!: Antifascist Dispatches from a World in Crisis.* His work has been featured in NBC News, The Baffler, Al Jazeera, The Daily Beast, Jacobin, In These Times, The Independent, Truthout, Political Research Associates, and Waging Nonviolence.

Sunny Megatron is an award-winning kink educator, certified sexuality educator and relationship coach, and media personality. She's the host and executive producer of the Showtime original television series *SEX with Sunny Megatron* and also co-hosts the AASECT award-winning *American Sex Podcast* and *Open Deeply Podcast*. In 2021, Sunny was named XBIZ Sexpert of the Year. Known for her one-of-a-kind build-your-own-adventure approach to sex, kink, and relationships, Sunny coined the BDSM community catchphrase "Kink is Customizable." In her sell-out workshops, her unique brand of "edutainment" seamlessly combines her humorous lecturing style, interactive exercises, and the latest sexuality research. Sunny's passion is helping others disarm shame and find their power through pleasure and play. Her first book, *Customizable Kink: A Strategic Guide to Adult Play*, was released in late 2022.

Wagatwe Wanjuki is a feminist theorist, educator, and digital strategist who focuses on gender-based violence prevention. As an award-winning anti-rape activist, she uses feminist theory to challenge myths and raise awareness on- and offline. Inspired by her own experience with campus sexual assault, Wagatwe advocates for better systemic responses and prevention. As a founding co-organizer of ED ACT NOW, she helped spur the Obama administration to create the Task Force to Protect Students Against Sexual Assault. Wagatwe lectures and leads workshops related to her activism with an intersectional lens and also serves as a research advisor on Sexual Health Against Right-wing Extremism at Suffolk University. Wagatwe's writing on sexual violence at the intersections of race and gender has been published by Bitch Media, Cosmopolitan, ESSENCE magazine, Teen Vogue, BuzzFeed News, and the New York Times, among others. Her activism has been featured in numerous books including *37 Words: Title IX and Fifty Years of Fighting Sex Discrimination* by Sherry Boschert. wagatwe.com and @wagatwe.

Yael R. Rosenstock Gonzalez is a queer, polyamorous Nuyorican (Puerto Rican New Yorker) Jewish pleasure activist (a term popularized by adrienne maree brown) who believes that sexual wellness and sexual liberation involve our whole selves. She centers identity and social positioning work, values self-exploration, and promotes intentional practice as a vehicle for desired shifts. Through her company, SexPositiveYou, Yael support clients in finding pleasurable, joyful, and positive experiences with self and sex. This includes connecting to embodied pleasure and pleasure techniques, improving confidence and self-worth, increasing emotional, physical, and sexual intimacy with partners, developing communication skills, setting and respecting boundaries, improving one's relationship with their body, and more. Yael is also an identity and belonging coach, business coach, researcher, and publisher. She is the the author of *An Introguide to a Sex Positive You* and the founder of Kaleidoscope Vibrations, LLC. sexpositiveyou.com and @yaelthesexgeek.

Zach Budd is a self-proclaimed nerd, sex geek, and consent junkie. He has been actively polyamorous for more than ten years. Zach became interested in consent as a topic as a personal research project. He is currently working towards a Master's of Social Work at the University of Houston to be of even more benefit to his community. Zach's personal research interests include intimate partner violence involving male victims, consent, consent education, consent culture building, alternative relationship styles and their history, self-care, consent and pleasure-based sexual education, consensual sex work and advocacy, and restorative and transformative justice. He is also the Gulf Coast Area advocate for the National Coalition for Sexual Freedom and a member of the board of directors for Loving More, the oldest polyamory nonprofit in the US. consentwarrior.com.